Answer Key to Accompany
Student Activities Manual

¡Trato hecho!
Spanish for Real Life
THIRD EDITION

John T. McMinn
Austin Community College

Nuria Alonso García
Providence College

Upper Saddle River, New Jersey 07458

Copyright © 2006 by Pearson Education, Inc.
Upper Saddle River, New Jersey 07458
All rights reserved

Printed in the United States of America
10 9 8 7 6 5 4 3 2 1

ISBN 0-13-191416-2

Capítulo 1 ¡A conocernos!

Tema 1 ¿Cómo te llamas? ¿Cómo estás?

1-1 ¿Cómo estás?

Scene A: Buenos días. ¿Cómo está? Estoy muy bien.

Scene B: Buenas tardes. ¿Cómo estás? Estoy mal.

1-2 Un nuevo estudiante.

1. Buenos	**4.** Se escribe	**7.** Y	**10.** Mucho
2. cómo	**5.** o	**8.** te llamas	**11.** Igualmente
3. Me llamo	**6.** con	**9.** *your own name*	

1-3. ¿Formal o familiar?

1. ¿Cómo te llamas?　　　**2.** ¿Cómo estás?　　　**3.** ¿De dónde eres?

1-4 ¿Y tú?

1. estás	**3.** Soy	**5.** Soy
2. Estoy	**4.** eres	**6.** soy

1-5 ¿Y Ud.?

— Buenos días, ¿cómo está Ud.?

— Estoy muy bien, gracias. Me llamo Federico Alfonso. Y Ud., ¿cómo se llama?

— Mucho gusto, señor Alfonso. Soy Cecilia Núñez.

— ¿De dónde es Ud., señora (señorita) Núñez?

— Soy de Montevideo. ¿Y Ud.?

— Yo soy de Buenos Aires.

1-6 ¿Cómo se escribe?

1. En inglés, *photo* **se escribe** con *ph* en vez de *f.*

2. En inglés, *biology* se escribe **con** *y* en vez de *ía.*

3. En inglés, *institution* se escribe con *t* en vez de *c* y **con** acento en la *o.*

4. En inglés, *romantic* **se escribe** sin **acento** en la *a* y **sin** la *o* final.

5. En inglés, *independent* **se escribe sin (la)** *i* y **sin la** *e* **final.**

1-8 Saludos.

1. b. Hola.	**3. a.** Soy Antonio.	**5. c.** Soy de Miami.
2. b. Estoy bien, gracias.	**4. a.** Me llamo Gabriela.	

1-10 Adjetivos

1. sentimental

2. optimista

3. responsable

4. liberal

5. egoísta

The answers to the second part of the activity will vary.

1-11 A lo personal.

Answers will vary.

Tema 2 Quiero presentarte a… / Quiero presentarle a…

1-12 Presentaciones.

1. Quiero presentar**te a mi madre**.

2. Quiero presentar**le a mi padre**.

3. Quiero presentar**te a mi compañera de clase**.

4. Quiero presentar**le a mi hermana**.

1-13 Comparaciones.

Some answers may vary.

1. Los republicanos son **menos** liberales **que** los demócratas.

2. Lance Armstrong es **más** atlético **que** Jennifer López.

3. Ted Koppel es **tan** intelectual **como** Peter Jennings.

4. Brad Pitt es **más** romántico **que** David Spade.

5. Ellen DeGeneres es **menos** seria **que** Hillary Clinton.

6. Jay Leno es **más** cómico **que** Ted Koppel.

1-14 Caracteres opuestos.

1. Enrique no es **extrovertido**. Es **tímido**.

2. Mónica es muy cómica. Enrique no es **cómico**. Es **serio**.

3. Enrique es muy pesimista. Mónica no es **pesimista**. Es **optimista**.

1-15 ¿Cómo son?

1. Mi padre es **intelectual**. No es muy **cómico**.

2. Mi hemana es **responsable**. No es muy **impulsiva**.

3. Mi hermano es **pesimista**. No es muy **ambicioso**.

4. Mi mejor amigo es **atlético**. No es muy **emocional**.

5. Mis padres son **religiosos**. No son muy **egoístas**.

6. Mis amigos son **liberales**. No son muy **tímidos**.

1-16 ¿Y tú?

The answers to the questions will vary.

1. somos; Sí (No), (no) somos compañeros de clase.

2. son; Mis profesores son…

3. eres; Soy de…

4. son; Mis padres son de…

5. es; Sí (No), mi mejor amigo(a) (no) es estudiante.

6. Eres; Sí (No), soy más (menos) extrovertido/a que mi mejor amigo/a.

7. Son; Sí (No), (no) somos muy serios/as.

1-18 ¿De quién habla?

1. a. su novio   **3. c.** ???   **5. a.** su novio

2. c. ???   **4. b.** su amiga   **6. c.** ???

1-19 Comparaciones.

1. b. falso Gabriela es más tímida que Alicia.   **4. a.** cierto

2. a. cierto   **5. b.** falso Alicia es menos seria que Gabriela.

3. b. falso Gabriela es menos divertida que Alicia.   **6. a.** cierto

1-20 A lo personal.

Answers will vary.

Tema 3 ¿Cómo es la universidad? ¿Qué clases tienes?

1-21 ¿En qué universidad?

1. Las residencias son más **feas** en la universidad B.   **4.** Los edificios son más **modernos** en la universidad B.

2. Las residencias son más **pequeñas** en la universidad A.   **5.** La cafetería es más **bonita** en la universidad A.

3. Los edificios son más **viejos** en la universidad A.   **6.** El gimnasio es más **pequeño** en la universidad B.

1-22 ¿Cómo son?

*The answers for **cierto/falso** will vary for different universities.*

1. La universidad no muy *grande*. Es **pequeña**.

2. Los edificios no son *feos*. Son **bonitos**.

3. La biblioteca no es *nueva*. Es **vieja**.

4. Las clases no son *difíciles*. Son **fáciles**.

5. La química no es *aburrida*. Es **interesante**.

6. Los profesores no son *perezosos*. Son **trabajadores**.

7. Los estudiantes no son *antipáticos*. Son **simpáticos**.

8. La clase de español no es *grande*. Es **pequeña**.

9. Las residencias no son *modernas*. Son **viejas**.

1-23 Disciplinas.

1. Es **la música** porque las otras clases son **lenguas**.

2. Es **la informática** porque las otras clases son **ciencias sociales**.

3. Es **el francés** porque las otras clases son **cursos técnicos**.

4. Es **la contabilidad** porque las otras clases son **bellas artes**.

1-24 Mis clases.

Answers will vary. The classes are as follows:

1. historia   **3.** química   **5.** música

2. español   **4.** informática

1-25 Preguntas.

Answers will vary.

1-27 ¿En qué clase?

1. a   **3.** b   **5.** a   **7.** a

2. b   **4.** a   **6.** b   **8.** b

1-29 ¿Compañeros de clase?

1. Él se llama **Pablo Morales** y ella se llama **Cristina Alfonso**.

2. Él es de **San Juan (Puerto Rico)** y ella es de **Nueva York**.

3. Este semestre él tiene clases de **filosofía, matemáticas, historia y física** y ella tiene clases de **economía, literatura, biología y filosofía**.

4. La clase favorita de él es **física**. Es **difícil** pero el profesor es **(muy) interesante**.

La clase favorita de ella es **filosofía** porque la profesora es **(muy) divertida y simpática**.

Tema 4 ¿Te gustan las clases? ¿Cuántos estudiantes hay?

1-30 Los hispanos.

a. once millones

b. dos punto **siete** millones

c. seis punto **siete** millones

d. dos punto **nueve** millones

e. treinta y nueve millones

f. el **trece** por ciento

g. el **sesenta y siete** por ciento

h. el **nueve** por ciento

i. el **cuatro** por ciento

j. el **treinta y cuatro** por ciento

k. el **cuarenta y tres** por ciento

1. e   **3.** I   **5.** a   **7.** b   **9.** f   **11.** k

2. g   **4.** h   **6.** c   **8.** d   **10.** j

1-31 ¿Cuál es tu número de teléfono?

1. Es el **siete, cincuenta y nueve, trece, treinta y tres.**

2. Es el **nueve, noventa, treinta y uno, cuarenta y uno.**

3. Es el **siete, cero siete, diecinueve, noventa y uno.**

4. Es el **seis, treinta y cinco, veinticuatro, cero nueve.**

5. Es el **ocho, treinta y ocho, noventa y siete, setenta.**

6. Es el **cuatro, cincuenta y cuatro, sesenta, veintiséis.**

1-32 ¿Le gusta(n)?

1. No le gusta la tarea.

2. Le gustan las clases sin mucha tarea.

3. Le gustan las actividades sociales.

4. No le gustan los exámenes.

5. No le gusta estudiar sola.

6. Le gusta estar con sus amigos.

1-33 Comparaciones.

1. Su novio es antipático.

2. Mis amigos son simpáticos.

3. Mis amigos son divertidos.

4. Su mejor amiga es egoísta.

5. Mi mejor amiga es muy paciente.

6. Mis profesores son muy interesantes.

7. Sus profesores son aburridos.

8. Mi hermana no es muy inteligente.

1-34 Preguntas.

Answers will vary.

1-36 Códigos secretos.

1. ¿Te gustan tus clases?   **2.** ¿Hay mucha tarea de español?

1-37 Matemáticas.

1. $8 + 5 = 13$

2. $14 + 15 = 29$

3. $19 + 11 = 30$

4. $20 + 12 = 32$

5. $33 + 7 = 40$

6. $44 + 14 = 58$

1-38 ¿Qué tal las clases?

1. No le gusta mucho la clase de informática porque es difícil y hay mucha tarea y muchos exámenes.

2. Le gustan las clases de ciencias políticas y de francés porque los estudiantes son simpáticos y los profesores son buenos.

3. Hay unos ochenta estudiantes en ciencias políticas. En informática hay veinticinco más o menos y en francés sólo hay quince.

Tema 5 ¿Qué hora es? ¿Cuándo son tus clases?

1-39 ¿Qué hora es?

1. Son las dos.

2. Son las dos y cuarto (quince).

3. Son las cinco y media (treinta).

4. Son las ocho menos cuarto (quince).

5. Son las once menos cinco.

1-40 ¡Estás confundido!

1. No, mañana es sábado.

2. No, esta tarea es para el jueves.

3. No, quiero estudiar para el examen el lunes.

4. No, el examen es el martes.

1-41 ¿Dónde está Ramón?

1. A las nueve menos cuarto (quince) de la mañana está en el autobús.

2. A las nueve de la mañana está en el autobús.

3. A las diez y cuarto (quince) de la mañana está en el trabajo.

4. Al mediodía (A las doce) está en el trabajo.

5. Al las tres y media (treinta) de la tarde está en el trabajo.

6. A las siete menos diez de la tarde está en casa.

1-42 Los días de clase.

1. los	**6.** y	**11.** los
2. en	**7.** a las	**12.** hay
3. por	**8.** e	**13.** el
4. por	**9.** Los	**14.** el
5. a la	**10.** de	

1-43 Preguntas.

Answers will vary.

1-45 Los acentos gráficos.

1. rancho	**5.** excelente	**9.** domingo
2. automático	**6.** hipócrita	**10.** sábado
3. teléfono	**7.** valiente	**11.** preocupado
4. negativo	**8.** miércoles	**12.** estás

1. fenomenal	**5.** profesor
2. oportunidad	**6.** útil
3. difícil	**7.** Martínez
4. estudiar	**8.** Gómez

1-46 Mi horario.

9:00 a.m., los lunes, miércoles y viernes: matemáticas

3:00 p.m., los lunes, miércoles y viernes: ciencias políticas

1:00 p.m., los martes y jueves: humanidades

2:30 p.m., los martes y jueves: psicología

5:00 – 7:00 p.m. (5:00 – 10:00 p.m.), los jueves y viernes: trabajo

Capítulo 2

Tema 1 ¿Qué hay?

2-1 ¿Qué hay en el salón de clase?

1. una pizarra	**5.** una ventana	**9.** un estante	**13.** un cuaderno
2. una profesora	**6.** un estudiante	**10.** un reloj	**14.** un lápiz
3. un escritorio	**7.** una estudiante	**11.** una mochila	**15.** un bolígrafo
4. una puerta	**8.** una silla	**12.** una calculadora	**16.** una computadora

2-2 En el escritorio.

1. una	**3.** unos	**5.** unos	**7.** unos	**9.** un	**11.** unos
2. un	**4.** unas	**6.** un	**8.** unas	**10.** una	**12.** un

Items found on a desk: 1, 3, 4, 5, 6, 7, 9, 12

2-3 ¿Qué hay?

1. Hay **una mochila** por **cuarenta y seis** dólares con **cincuenta** centavos.

2. Hay **un reloj** por **cien** dólares.

3. Hay **una silla** por **setenta y nueve** dólares con **noventa y nueve** centavos.

4. Hay **un cuaderno** por **cuatro** dólares con **treinta y nueve** centavos.

5. Hay **un lápiz** por **quince** centavos.

2-4 ¿Qué necesitamos hacer?

The following endings should be crossed out.

1. la oración	**3.** la ventana	**5.** una calculadora	**7.** el estante
2. una silla	**4.** a la pizarra	**6.** la puerta	**8.** el reloj

2-5 ¿Y tú?

Answers will vary.

2-7 ¿Qué hay y dónde?

1. a	**3.** a	**5.** a	**7.** b	**9.** a
2. b	**4.** b	**6.** a	**8.** a	**10.** a

Tema 2 ¿Qué hay cerca de la universidad?

2-10 ¿Qué hay?

1. la librería	**3.** mi restaurante favorito	**5.** el cine
2. el estadio	**4.** el club nocturno	

2-11 En el centro estudiantil.

1. Juan está **entre** Daniel y Arturo.

2. Juan, Daniel y Arturo están **detrás** de Mari y Teresa.

3. Marta está **a la izquierda** de Silvia y no hay nadie *(anybody)* a su derecha.

4. La computadora está **encima** del escritorio **enfrente** de Mari.

5. Daniel está cerca de la entrada pero Ricardo está **lejos**.

6. La entrada está **delante** de Marta y Silvia.

2-12 ¿Dónde está?

1. Mi madre **está en un parque**.

2. Mis padres **están en un restaurante**.

3. Mi novio y yo **estamos un club (nocturno)**.

4. Mis amigos y yo **estamos en un cine**.

5. Yo **estoy en una tienda (de ropa)** / **un centro comercial**.

6. Mis amigos y yo **estamos en un café**.

7. Mi padre **está en un supermercado**.

2-13 ¿Dónde está?

1. está	**4.** estoy	**7.** estamos	**10.** hay	**13.** está
2. Estoy	**5.** está	**8.** está	**11.** estoy	**14.** está
3. hay	**6.** Estamos	**9.** Hay	**12.** están	**15.** están

2-15 ¿Cómo se pronuncia?

The following ds should be underlined.

— ¿Qué **d**ías trabaja E**d**uar**d**o?

— Todos los **d**ías **d**e la semana menos los sábados y los **d**omingos.

— ¿**D**ón**d**e está E**d**uar**d**o todo el **d**ía los sábados?

— Está en el esta**d**io para un parti**d**o **d**e fútbol.

— ¿**D**ón**d**e está la tien**d**a de ropa don**d**e trabaja? ¿Está a la **d**erecha o a la izquierda **d**el supermercado?

— Está **d**etrás **d**el supermercado y al lado de un restaurante de comida italiana.

2-16 En mi cuarto.

1. *On the books on the shelf.*

2. *On the plant in front of the window.*

3. *On the desk to the left of the door.*

4. *On the chair in front of the desk.*

5. *On the door near the desk*

6. *On the window to the right of the door.*

7. *On the computer under the shelf.*

8. *On the shelf to the left of the door.*

Tema 3 ¿Están listos o necesitan más tiempo?

2-17 ¿Cómo están?

1. Mi hermano es un poco perezoso y siempre **está cansado**.

2. Mi compañera de clase **está enferma**.

3. Hay mucho trabajo hoy y mi padre y sus colegas **están ocupados**. Mi padre **está listo** para su presentación.

4. Mis amigos y yo no **estamos interesados** en la película porque no es muy interesante. **Estamos aburridos**.

5. Mi mejor amiga y su novio **están estupendos**.

2-18 ¿Dónde están?

1. **Son** las diez de la mañana y mi hermano **está** en la cama *(bed)*.

2. Mi compañera de clase **está** en el hospital. **Es** muy buena estudiante.

3. Mi padre y sus colegas **están** en el trabajo. **Son** muy trabajadores.

4. Mis amigos y yo **estamos** en el cine. **Somos** buenos amigos.

5. Mi mejor amiga no **es** muy tímida. Su novio y ella **están** en un club nocturno.

2-19 Nuevos amigos.

1. estamos	4. eres	7. Soy	10. es	13. es	16. estoy
2. Soy	5. soy	8. son	11. es	14. Estás	17. está
3. estás	6. está	9. estoy	12. estoy	15. son	

2-20 Mucho gusto.

The answers to the questions will vary. The verbs in the questions are:

1. estás	2. Eres	3. son	4. eres	5. es	6. Está

2-22 ¿Entienden Uds.?

1. **b.** No, necesitamos más tiempo.

2. **a.** Sí, tengo una pregunta.

3. **a.** No comprendo.

4. **b.** No sé cómo se dice.

5. **a.** No sé. No comprendo la pregunta.

6. **a.** Estamos confundidos. ¿Qué significa *pueden*?

7. **b.** ¿Cuál es la tarea para hoy?

8. **a.** ¿Cómo se escribe *está*, con acento o sin acento?

2-23 ¿Cómo están y cómo son?

1. **b.** Bien	3. **a.** de aquí	5. **a.** grande	7. **a.** simpáticos
2. **a.** bajos	4. **b.** en mi cuarto	6. **b.** cerca de mi casa	8. **b.** nerviosos

2-24 ¿Y tú?

Answers will vary.

Tema 4 ¿Qué te gusta hacer después de clase?

2-25 ¿Qué haces?

1. — ¿**Miras** mucho la tele sola en casa los fines de semana?

   — Los viernes, sí, generalmente, **miro** la tele porque mi novio trabaja, pero los sábados me gusta ir a

   bailar con él.

2. — ¿**Bailan** bien?

   — Yo **bailo** bien pero él **baila** mal.

3. — A veces, ¿**toman** algo en un café con otros amigos?

   — Sí, a veces, **tomamos** algo con mi hermana y su novio.

4. — ¿Tu hermano no **pasa** mucho tiempo contigo?

   — A veces, mi hermano y su compañero de cuarto **pasan** los viernes conmigo, pero no mucho

   porque a mi novio no le gusta.

5. — ¿Tus amigos y tú **escuchan** más música latina o más música rock?

   — **Escuchamos** más música rock.

6. — ¿**Compras** mucha ropa para salir con los amigos?

   — No, casi nunca **compro** ropa nueva porque no tengo dinero *(money)*.

7. — ¿**Trabajas** mucho en casa los fines de semana?

   — Me gusta **trabajar** en el jardín *(the garden)* los sábados por la tarde.

2-26 ¿Con frecuencia?

1. Mis amigos y yo **casi siempre** pasamos los sábados juntos, pero sus amigos pasan los sábados con él

   una vez al mes.

2. Él mira la televisión **con frecuencia** los viernes por la noche, pero yo **casi nunca** miro la tele los viernes.

3. Yo **nunca** estudio los fines de semana, pero él estudia **todos los fines de semana**.

4. Mis amigos y yo bailamos en un club **una vez a la semana**, pero sus amigos bailan **una o dos veces al año**.

5. **A veces** yo regreso muy tarde *(late)* a casa los sábados, pero él **casi nunca** regresa tarde a casa.

2-27 En clase.

Answers will vary.

2-28 Mis amigos y yo.

1. estoy	**3.** paso	**5.** llega	**7.** comer	**9.** tocan	**11.** regreso	**13.** miramos
2. estudio	**4.** trabaja	**6.** preparamos	**8.** ir	**10.** tomar	**12.** descanso	**14.** necesitamos

2-30 ¿En clase o después de clase?

1. a   **2.** b   **3.** b   **4.** a   **5.** a   **6.** b   **7.** b   **8.** a   **9.** b

2-31 ¿Con qué frecuencia?

Answers will vary.

2-32 El día de Ramón.

1. b. casi todos los días	**3. a.** casi nunca	**5. b.** todos los días	**7. a.** nunca
2. a. nunca	**4. b.** con frecuencia	**6. b.** dos o tres veces al mes	**8. a.** una vez al mes

Tema 5 ¿Cómo pasas el día?

2-33 Los fines de semana.

1. Qué	3. Por qué	5. Cómo	7. Cuántas
2. quién	4. Cuál	6. Dónde	8. Cuándo

2-34 ¿Y tú?

Answers will vary.

2-35 ¿Qué o cuál?

1. Qué	3. Cuál	5. Qué	7. qué
2. Cuál	4. Qué	6. Cuál	8. Qué

2-36 ¿Y tú?

Answers will vary.

2-37 ¿Cuál es la pregunta?

1. — **¿Dónde está Lorenzo?**
   — Está en su cuarto.
   — **¿Con quién baila?**
   — No baila con nadie. Baila solo.
   — **¿Cómo baila?**
   — Baila muy mal.

2. — **¿Con quién estudia Patricio?**
   — Estudia con Aura.
   — **¿Dónde están?**
   — Están en la biblioteca.
   — **¿Qué estudian?**
   — Estudian historia.
   — **¿Por qué estudian?**
   — Estudian porque hay un examen el lunes.

2-39 Preguntas.

1. b. cuánta	**4. b.** cómo	**7. b.** qué
2. b. dónde	**5. b.** con quién	**8. a.** dónde
3. a. por qué	**6. a.** quiénes	**9. a.** cuántas

Capítulo 3 En casa

Tema 1 ¿Dónde vives? ¿Cuál es tu dirección?

3-1 ¿Qué hay en la casa?

1. un árbol	6. una mesa	11. una chimenea	16. un coche / un carro
2. un microondas	7. un comedor	12. un baño	17. una planta
3. una cocina	8. un sofá	13. un dormitorio	18. un jardín
4. una nevera	9. una sala	14. una cama	19. una piscina
5. una silla	10. un televisor	15. un garaje	20. una flor

3-2 La cocina está…

1. nevera	3. sofá	5. jardín
2. baño	4. cocina	6. sala

3-3 Dinero internacional.

1. cien; ciento veintiséis
2. cuatrocientos; ciento treinta y cinco
3. seis millones; tres mil ciento treinta
4. siete mil; ochocientos
5. novecientos; ciento quince

3-4 ¿Cuánto pagas?

1. cien
2. doscientos cincuenta; trescientos
3. mil seiscientos
4. cinco mil quinientos

3-5 ¿Y tú?
Answers will vary.

3-7 Anuncios.

1. piscina; 900
2. baño; 575
3. cocina; comedor; 650
4. dormitorios; 1200

3-8 ¿Dónde vives?
Answers will vary.

Tema 2 ¿Cómo es tu cuarto?

3-9 ¿Qué hay?

1. cómoda	3. impresora	5. pared	7. escritorio
2. suelo	4. cama	6. un reproductor de DVD	8. lámpara

3-10 De colores.

1. azul
2. amarilla
3. verde
4. blanca
5. azul
6. roja

3-11 El cuarto de Juan y el cuarto de Mario.

1. armario   **2.** estante   **3.** gatos   **4.** lados   **5.** pinturas   **6.** limpio

3-12 ¿Qué tienen?

1. Mis; tenemos   **2.** tiene; su   **3.** tienen; sus; tengo; mi   **4.** tenemos; nuestro

3-13 ¿Y tú?

Answers will vary.

3-15 En mi cuarto hay...

The following items should be marked:

una alfombra, pinturas, dos ventanas, muebles bonitos.

3-16 ¿Cierto?

Answers will vary.

3-17 Mi compañero.

1. tenemos

2. televisor; reproductor de DVD

3. ordenada

4. por todos lados

5. tengo coche; coche

6. escritorio; computadora

Tema 3 ¿Cómo es tu familia?

3-18 La familia de Alicia.

1. Mi abuela   **4.** Mi tía   **7.** Mi hermana

2. Mi madre   **5.** Mi tío   **8.** Mi prima

3. Mi padre   **6.** Mi hermano   **9.** Mi sobrina

3-19 Mi familia.

1. Me llamo   **4.** hermanas   **7.** abuelos   **10.** hijos

2. tengo   **5.** hermanos   **8.** tíos   **11.** se parecen

3. madre   **6.** gato   **9.** casados   **12.** en el carácter

3-20 ¿Cómo son?

1. El abuelo Francisco usa gafas.

2. El tío Emilio tiene bigote.

3. La prima Rosa tiene el pelo largo.

4. El tío Emilio es de mediana edad.

5. El abuelo Francisco, el primo Eduardo, y el tío Emilio tienen el pelo corto.

6. El primo Eduardo es joven.

3-21 Contrarios.

1. No, **tienen una hermana menor.**

2. No, **el padre de René es bajo.**

3. No, **tiene unos abuelos jóvenes.**

4. No, **Adriana es peor que su hermano en matemáticas.**

5. No, **la tía de Antonio está delgada.**

3-22 Quiero tener clases mejores.

1. Quiero tener clases más interesantes que ahora. / Quiero tener clases tan interesantes como ahora.

2. Quiero tener clases más grandes que ahora. / Quiero tener clases menos grandes que ahora. / Quiero tener clases tan grandes como ahora.

3. Quiero tener menos tarea en mis clases que ahora. / Quiero tener tanta tarea en mis clases como ahora.

4. Quiero tener profesores mejores que ahora. / Quiero tener profesores tan buenos como ahora.

3-24 La familia de Pablo.

1. grande	**3.** mayor	**5.** físico	**7.** corto	**9.** alto
2. se llaman	**4.** menor	**6.** se parece	**8.** delgado	**10.** carácter

3-25 No es lógico.

1. Generalmente los hijos menores son menos altos que los hijos mayores.

2. Generalmente los abuelos son más canosos que los padres.

3. Generalmente las hijas tienen el pelo menos corto que los hijos.

4. Generalmente los hijos se parecen más a los padres que a los tíos.

5. Generalmente los hijos trabajan menos que los padres.

3-26 Juan y Mario.

1. mayor	**3.** menos alto	**5.** más largo
2. más simpático	**4.** mejor	**6.** menos gordo

Tema 4 ¿Qué haces los días de clase?

3-27 ¿Qué hace Ángela?

1. come; comen

2. lee

3. corre; corren

4. asiste; aprenden

5. come; comen

6. escribe; lee

7. ve; ven

3-28 Los días de clase.

1. como   **2.** Leo   **3.** bebo   **4.** asisto   **5.** aprendo   **6.** escribo   **7.** veo   **8.** corro

3-29 ¿Con qué frecuencia?

Answers will vary.

3-30 No comprendemos.

1. comprendemos	**3.** Asisten	**5.** Escriben	**7.** Deben
2. vemos	**4.** aprendemos	**6.** leemos	**8.** creen

3-32 ¿Cómo se pronuncia?

The following bs and vs should be underlined.

— <u>V</u>ivo en una casa cerca de la universidad.

— Escribo correos electrónicos con <u>b</u>astante frecuencia.

— Me gusta mi <u>b</u>arrio. Hay <u>v</u>ecinos <u>b</u>uenos, un parque y muchos cafés.

— <u>B</u>ebo café por las mañanas, <u>v</u>eo la televisión por las tardes.

— <u>V</u>endo mis libros en <u>v</u>erano (*summer*) después del final del semestre.

3-33 ¿En clase o después de clase?

1. b	**3.** b	**5.** b	**7.** b	**9.** b	**11.** a
2. a	**4.** b	**6.** a	**8.** a	**10.** a	**12.** b

3-34 A veces...

Answers will vary.

Tema 5 ¿Qué haces los sábados?

3-35 Los días de semana o los fines de semana.

1. Comen con amigos en la cafetería los días de semana.

2. Asisten a clase los días de semana.

3. Salen a bailar los fines de semana.

4. Asisten a un concierto los fines de semana.

5. Traen preguntas a la clase los días de semana.

6. Salen al cine los fines de semana.

7. Corren en el parque después de clase los días de semana.

3-36 Los fines de semana de Elena.

1. hace ejercicio; hacen ejercicio	**3.** oye	**5.** hacen un viaje; hace un viaje
2. asisten a un concierto; asiste	**4.** salen; hace	

3-37 Los sábados de Andrés.

1. salgo   2. asistimos   3. vemos   4. hago   5. pongo   6. leo   7. hacemos   8. salimos

3-38 ¿Cuál es la pregunta?

1. Generalmente, ¿bebes mucho café?

   Generalmente, bebo **poco** café.

2. Generalmente, ¿asistes con amigos a conciertos?

   Asisto a conciertos con amigos **los sábados por la noche** generalmente.

3. Generalmente, ¿cuándo haces tu tarea los fines de semana?

   Los fines de semana hago mi tarea **los domingos por la noche** generalmente.

4. Generalmente, ¿oyes mucha música?

   Generalmente, oigo **mucha** música.

5. Generalmente, ¿escribes muchos correos electrónicos?

   Generalmente escribo **pocos** correos electrónicos.

6. ¿Haces viajes los fines de semana?

   Los fines de semana hago viajes **con frecuencia.**

7. Generalmente, ¿pones música para bailar en tu dormitorio?

   A veces pongo música para bailar en mi dormitorio.

8. Generalmente, ¿ves la televisión por la mañana?

   Generalmente veo la televisión **por la mañana.**

3-39 ¿Y tú?

Answers will vary.

3-41 ¿Cómo se pronuncia?

The following gs should be underlined.

— Mi gato está encima del garaje.

— En general, comprendo las preguntas del profesor de inglés.

— Mi clase favorita es la clase de biología con la profesora García.

— Germán es el mejor estudiante de la clase.

— Salgo al cine con mis amigos los sábados.

— A veces hago un viaje con Gema a la playa.

3-42 ¿Qué hacemos el sábado?

Marta quiere...: salir a un restaurante; hacer una fiesta en casa; hacer un viaje a la playa.

Antonio quiere...: pasar el sábado en casa; hacer la tarea; ver el partido de fútbol en la televisión; estar en casa y oír música.

3-43 Preguntas.

1. hago   2. tengo   3. traen   4. hacen   5. vemos

Capítulo 4

Tema 1 ¿Adónde vas en tus ratos libres?

4-1 ¿Adónde van?

1. Mis amigos y yo vamos a un restaurante.

2. Mis amigos van al centro comercial. / Mis amigos van a un centro comercial.

3. ¿Vas al gimnasio?

4. ¿Van al cine?

5. Voy al parque.

6. Vamos al café. / Vamos a un café.

7. ¿Vas al lago?

4-2 ¿Y ustedes?

Answers will vary.

4-3 ¿Qué hacen allí?

1. Nosotros vamos a la clase de español para aprender a hablar español.

2. Mis padres van al trabajo para trabajar.

3. Muchos estudiantes van a la cafetería para comer.

4. Algunos estudiantes van al gimnasio para levantar pesas.

5. Después de clase, yo voy a mi casa para descansar.

6. A veces, mis amigos y yo vamos al café para tomar algo.

4-4 Entrevista.

Answers will vary. The verb forms in the questions are:

1. van   **2.** vas   **3.** van   **4.** va   **5.** van

4-6 ¿Por qué no vamos a...?

1. el lago	**4.** el cine	**7.** el parque
2. el gimnasio	**5.** el café	**8.** un club
3. la montaña	**6.** el centro comercial	**9.** la casa

4-7 Planes.

1. Ella va **al supermercado** porque tiene que **comprar** algunas cosas.

2. Ella no tiene mucho tiempo porque **van a la iglesia** esta tarde.

3. Después de eso, van a ir **(a comer y) al cine** porque él quiere ver una **nueva película extranjera.**

4. Van a comer en un restaurante de comida mexicana que está **al lado del cine.**

4-8 Entrevista.

Answers will vary.

Tema 2 ¿Qué tiempo hace? ¿Qué vas a hacer?

4-9 ¿Qué tiempo hace?

1. Mis hermanos y yo **vamos** a **Colombia**.

   Allí, hace **sol** generalmente.

2. Yo también **voy** a **Ecuador**.

   Hoy el cielo está **nublado**.

3. Mis hermanos **van** a **Perú**. Necesitan paraguas porque allí **llueve**.

4. ¿Quién **va** a **Bolivia**? Allí no hace tanto frío ahora, sino **fresco**.

5. Nadie **va** a **Paraguay**.

   En julio, a veces hace mucho **viento**.

6. Y tú, ¿**vas** a **Chile** con tu familia?

   Dicen que hace mucho **frío** a veces en julio.

7. ¿**Van** Uds. a **(la) Argentina** también?

   Pueden esquiar porque **nieva**.

8. ¿Por qué quieres **ir** a **Uruguay**?

   El cielo está **nublado** y hace muy **mal** tiempo ahora.

4-10 Los meses.

1. septiembre   2. octubre   3. marzo   4. abril   5. julio   6. agosto   7. diciembre   8. enero

4-11 ¿Cuándo nacieron?

1. Jennifer López nació el veinticuatro de julio del año mil novecientos setenta.

2. Salma Hayak nació el dos de septiembre del año mil novecientos sesenta y ocho.

3. Sammy Sosa nació el doce de noviembre del año mil novecientos sesenta y ocho.

4-12 ¿Qué van a hacer?

1. Si hace sol y calor este fin de semana, **vamos a tomar el sol en la playa**.

2. Si llueve esta tarde, **voy a necesitar mi paraguas**.

3. Si está muy nublado, pero no hace frío, **va a llover**.

4. Si nieva mucho este invierno, vamos a **esquiar**.

5. Si no hace frío este invierno, no **va a nevar**

4-13 ¿Cuándo?

Answers will vary.

4-15 Depende del tiempo.

1. esquiar en la montaña   3. jugar al fútbol americano   5. ir al lago

2. pasar la tarde en casa   4. comer en el comedor

4-16 ¿Adónde vas?

1. h   2. i   3. a   4. k   5. j   6. c   7. f   8. e   9. b

Tema 3 ¿Qué quieres hacer? ¿Puedes…?

4-17 ¿Quién?

1. repito	5. quiero	9. sirve	13. cuenta
2. encuentro	6. puedo	10. pedimos	14. jugamos
3. duermo	7. pierdo	11. prefiere	15. dice
4. empiezo	8. almorzamos	12. tiene	16. vuelvo
			17. viene

4-18 ¿Qué quieren hacer?

1. Después de la exposición, mis padres **van** a un restaurante porque **quieren cenar**.

2. Mis amigos y yo **vamos** al lago mañana porque **queremos hacer esquí acuático**.

3. Mis abuelos **van** al teatro porque **quieren ver una obra**.

4. Mi prima **va** a la montaña para las vacaciones porque **quiere esquiar**.

5. Esta tarde **voy** al parque porque **quiero correr**.

6. No **voy** a la oficina hoy porque no **quiero trabajar**.

7. Ahora mi mejor amigo y yo **vamos** al café porque **queremos tomar algo**.

4-19. Una invitación.

1. Puedes	4. tengo	7. tienes
2. quiero	5. Podemos	8. puedo
3. puedo	6. prefieres	9. prefiero

4-20 Hay mucho que hacer.

1. dormimos	6. juegan	11. entiende
2. preferimos	7. quiero	12. pueden
3. piensan	8. puedo	13. prefieren
4. almuerzo	9. dicen	14. pueden
5. encuentro	10. pienso	

4-22 ¿Respuestas?

1. a las nueve de la mañana   3. a un café   5. a la seis y media

2. en la cafetería de la universidad   4. en un café

4-23 Una invitación.

1. Esta noche él quiere asistir a **un concierto** del grupo *Los Lobos,* pero ella no **puede** porque tiene que acompañar a sus padres a **la casa de sus abuelos**.

2. Mañana por la tarde, él quiere **ir al cine,** pero ella no puede porque **tiene que** trabajar.

3. Ella **puede** salir mañana por la noche porque **vuelve** del trabajo a las seis.

4. Ella prefiere comer en un restaurante de **comida italiana** y después van a ir a **bailar**.

4-24 Entrevista.

Answers will vary.

Tema 4 ¿Qué están haciendo ahora?

4-25 Una fiesta.

1. Están tocando música.

2. Están bailando con sus novios.

3. Están mirando (viendo) el partido de voléibol.

4. Está hablando de su trabajo con un hombre que le gusta mucho.

5. Está escuchando (oyendo) a una mujer aburrida hablar de su trabajo.

6. Están tomando (bebiendo) un refresco.

7. Están jugando al voléibol.

8. Está contando un chiste.

4-26. ¿Quién?

1. Nadie está comiendo pastel con helado.

2. Dos mujeres están poniendo la mesa.

3. Varias personas están jugando en la piscina.

4. Nadie está sacando una foto.

5. Casi todos están haciendo algo.

6. Unas personas están tomando el sol.

4-27 ¿Qué están haciendo?

1. Estoy esquiando.

2. Mi amigo está nadando.

3. ¿Están jugando al tenis?

4. Mi hermano está levantando pesas.

5. Estamos viendo una obra de teatro (aeróbico).

6. Estoy haciendo ejercicio

7. ¿Estás tomando el sol?

4-29 ¿Qué están haciendo?

1. i **2.** c **3.** d **4.** a **5.** b **6.** e **7.** h **8.** g

4-30 ¿Quién es?

a. 2   **b.** 1   **c.** 4   **d.** 5   **e.** 3

1. Mi compañera de cuarto y yo **estamos jugando al tenis en al parque.**
2. Mi amigo **esta estudiando italiano** porque **hace un viaje** a Italia.
3. Mi padre **está paseando** solo **en el parque.**
4. Mi sobrino **está nadando en la piscina.**
5. Mi compañera de clase **está cantando** *La Bamba* con **el profesor.**

Tema 5 ¿Quieres ir al café?

4-31 En el café.

1. vino
2. cerveza
3. agua

4. jugo
5. café
6. chocolate

7. té
8. bocadillo, jamón
9. helado, vainilla

4-32 ¿Hambre o sed?

1. **¿Quieres un bocadillo (de jamón y queso)? ¿Tienes hambre?**
2. **Quiero (una) limonada**, por favor. **Tengo sed.**
3. **Queremos (una) ensalada**, por favor. **Tenemos hambre.**
4. Los niños **quieren pizza. Tienen hambre.**
5. Nadie **quiere (un) helado (de vainilla). Nadie tiene hambre.**

4-33 ¿Qué quiere?

1. No, no quiere nada con azúcar.
2. No, no quiere (ni) queso ni jamón.
3. No, nunca toma cafeína. / No, no toma nunca cafeína.

Mi amigo prefiere (**una**) **ensalada.**

4-34 Expresiones negativas.

1. No, no quiero tomar ni agua mineral ni limonada.
2. No, no quiero chocolate con mi helado tampoco.
3. No, no juego con ningún amigo del barrio.
4. No, nadie viene esta tarde a jugar conmigo. / No, no viene nadie esta tarde a jugar conmigo.
5. No, nunca duermo una siesta por la tarde. / No, no duermo nunca una siesta por la tarde.

4-35 Entrevista.

Answers will vary. The words in the questions should be:

1. algo   **2.** ninguna, ni   **3.** alguien   **4.** nadie   **5.** algunos

4-37 ¿Tienen hambre o tienen sed?

1. a   **2.** b   **3.** b   **4.** a   **5.** a   **6.** a   **7.** b   **8.** b

4-38 En el restaurante.

1. alguien   **2.** ni… ni   **3.** nadie   **4.** algunas   **5.** alguien   **6.** algunas   **7.** nadie   **8.** ni… ni

Capítulo 5

Tema 1 ¿Qué haces los sábados?

5-1 Los sábados de Noemí.

1. Se despierta a las diez.
2. Se levanta a las diez y media.
3. Se ducha por la mañana.
4. Se lava los dientes.
5. Se relaja en casa por la tarde.
6. Se maquilla para salir.
7. Se encuentra con los amigos en el centro.
8. Se acuesta tarde.

5-2 Los días de clase y los sábados.

1. me levanto temprano; me levanto tarde
2. comemos en la cafetería; nos encontramos en un restaurante en el centro
3. me visto para ir a clase; me maquillo para salir
4. escribimos ensayos por la tarde; asistimos a un concierto

5-3 ¿Reflexivo o no reflexivo?

1. se queda
2. despierta
3. se viste
4. se divierten
5. baña
6. se sienta
7. se llaman
8. se siente
9. acuesta
10. se acuesta

5-4 Rutinas distintas.

1. se levanta
2. me quedo
3. me relajo
4. me divierto
5. me voy

5-6 Entrevista.

1. me lavo
2. me voy
3. nos llamamos
4. me quedo
5. nos encontramos
6. me acuesto

5-7 ¿Qué haces los sábados?

Answers will vary.

5-8 No es lógico.

1. Me lavo la cara y me maquillo.
2. Me baño y me voy a la universidad.
3. Cenamos y nos relajamos después de la cena.
4. Me quedo un poco en la cama y me levanto a las diez y media.
5. Me visto para salir y mis amigos y yo nos encontramos en un restaurante.

Tema 2 ¿Qué haces con los amigos y los seres queridos?

5-9 Novios.

1. Alma y Rafael se llevan bien.

2. Alma y Rafael se ven casi todos los días.

3. Estela y Pedro se enojan todos los sábados.

4. Alma y Rafael se besan antes de despedirse.

5. Estela y Pedro se pelean con frecuencia.

6. Alma y Rafael se van a casar algún día.

7. Alma y Rafael se encuentran en un café después del trabajo.

8. Estela y Pedro no se hablan mucho.

9. Alma y Rafael se comunican por correo electrónico a menudo.

5-10 ¿Qué hacen cuando...?

1. nos abrazamos

2. se hablan

3. nos reconciliamos

4. se dan la mano

5. se pelean

6. nos encontramos en un café

5-11 ¿Qué van a hacer las amigas?

1. Yo tengo que levantarme temprano el sábado.

2. Yo no puedo relajarme.

3. Tú puedes quedarte en casa toda la mañana.

4. Yo tengo que irme temprano.

5. Tú vas a divertirte con los amigos.

6. Yo voy a sentirme muy triste en el trabajo.

5-12 ¿Qué están haciendo?

1. se está duchando/está duchándose

2. se está vistiendo/está vistiéndose

3. se están besando/están besándose

4. se están pidiendo/están pidiéndose

5. se están peleando/están peleándose

5-13 Alma y Rafael.

1. Alma y Rafael se están hablando/están hablándose por teléfono.

2. Alma y Rafael se están abrazando/están abrazándose y se están besando/están besándose.

3. Alma y Rafael se están peleando/están peleándose.

4. Alma y Rafael se están despidiendo/están despidiéndose.

5-15 Mi mejor amigo y yo.

Answers will vary.

5-16 El Club Trapecio.

1. puedes encontrarte

2. me voy a acostar

3. tengo que levantarme

4. debes quedarte

5. Van a verse

6. vamos a divertirnos

Tema 3 ¿Qué te vas a poner?

5-17 De moda.

1. un vestido
2. una blusa
3. una falda
4. una bolsa
5. un abrigo
6. unas botas
7. una chaqueta
8. unas corbatas
9. una camisa
10. unos pantalones
11. un sombrero
12. un suéter

5-18 Ropa para cada ocasión.

1. traje de baño
2. tenis
3. traje / vestido
4. sombrero / botas
5. impermeable
6. calcetines

5-19 ¿Éste o ése?

1. estos; aquéllos
2. esa; ésta
3. este; aquél
4. estas; ésas
5. aquella, ésta

5-20 ¡Qué caro!

1. Esos
2. Aquel; éste
3. ésa
4. Aquel; éste
5. esa
6. aquellos; éstos

5-21 Intérprete.

1. Necesita una blusa de seda y una falda de lana.
2. No, no le gusta esta falda negra, prefiere esa falda gris.
3. Sí, esta blusa azul es perfecta.
4. No, no le gustan esos zapatos azules, le gustan aquellos zapatos rosados (rosa).

5-23 ¿Lógico o ilógico?

1. ilógico
2. ilógico
3. lógico
4. ilógico
5. lógico
6. ilógico
7. lógico
8. lógico

5-24 ¿Cuál prefieres?

1. No, prefiero ésas.
2. No, prefiero ésos.
3. No, prefiero ése.
4. No, prefiero ésa.
5. No, prefiero ésos.

5-25 Entrevista.

1. traje
2. abrigo
3. traje de baño
4. tenis
5. pantalones cortos

Tema 4 ¿Cuánto cuesta?

5-26 En el escaparate.

1. el cliente/la clienta
2. los probadores
3. el dependiente/la dependienta
4. el efectivo
5. la caja
6. la tarjeta de crédito
7. la tarjeta de débito

5-27 ¿A qué se refiere?

1. b   **2.** a   **3.** e   **4.** c   **5.** d

5-28 ¿En qué puedo servirle?

1. lo   **3.** La   **5.** la   **7.** Los   **9.** la

2. la   **4.** Las   **6.** los   **8.** la   **10.** las

5-29 ¿Te los vas a llevar?

1. No, no **las aceptan en todas las tiendas.**   **4.** Sí, **me la pongo.**   **5.** Sí, generalmente **los llevo.**

2. Sí, **me lo voy a llevar/voy a llevármelo.**   3. No, no **lo uso mucho.**   **6.** No, no **la voy a llevar/voy a llevarla.**

5-31 No, nunca...

Answers will vary.

5-32 En la zapatería.

1. lo   **2.** los   **3.** lo   **4.** se los   **5.** lo   **6.** la   **7.** me los   **8.** las

Tema 5 ¿Para quién es?

5-33 ¿Adónde vas para...?

1. la joyería   **2.** la zapatería   **3.** la peluquería   **4.** la pastelería   **5.** la librería

5-34 No tienes mucho dinero.

1. regalo   **2.** cadena   **3.** cartera   **4.** gorra   **5.** anillo   **6.** descuento

5-35 ¿Por o para?

1. c   **2.** e   **3.** f   **4.** b   **5.** a   **6.** d   **7.** h   **8.** g

5-36 Hola, Conchita, soy Paz.

1. para   **3.** por   **5.** para   **7.** por   **9.** para

2. por   **4.** por   **6.** para   **8.** para   **10.** por

5-37 Fragmentos.

1. Marta se viste para salir a cenar con su amigo Antonio.

2. Marta está sorprendida por la invitación de Antonio.

3. Marta y Antonio se hablan por teléfono para decidir adónde van a cenar.

4. Marta conoce un restaurante famoso por su pescado.

5. Antonio va a hacer una reserva para las siete y media.

6. Antonio va a pasar por Marta a las siete.

5-39 ¿La carnicería o la pescadería?

1. **a** la carnicería   3. **a** la zapatería   5. **a** la librería

2. **a** la pastelería   4. **a** la joyería   6. **a** la pescadería

5-40 ¿Y tú?

Answers will vary.

5-41 Desacuerdos.

María José quiere...: quedarse en casa para descansar; pasar por casa de sus padres para cenar; hacer compras por Internet; ir a la zapatería.

Alejandro quiere...: salir por la noche a bailar; cenar en un restaurante en el centro; ir de compras al centro comercial; pasar por la joyería.

Capítulo 6

Tema 1 ¿Adónde fuiste de vacaciones?

6-1 Descanso de primavera.

En Nueva York, yo…

Visité la Estatua de la Libertad.

Vi tres obras de teatro.

Tomé el metro más que el autobús

Corrí cada mañana en el Parque Central.

Fui a varios museos.

Asisití a un partido de los *Knicks*.

En Cancún, ¿tú…?

¿Nadaste mucho?

¿Hablaste sólo en español?

¿Probaste la comida del Yucatán?

¿Fuiste a la playa todos los días?

¿Tomaste el sol todo el tiempo?

¿Saliste en velero?

¿Pescaste en el mar?

¿Visitaste las ruinas mayas cerca de allí?

¿Te alojaste en un hotel cerca de la playa?

6-2 Un turista enfermo.

1. Sus amigos pasaron un día estupendo, pero Oswaldo pasó un día muy aburrido.

2. Sus amigos tomaron un taxi al centro, pero Oswaldo tomó antibióticos.

3. Sus amigos vieron muchos sitios históricos, pero Oswaldo vio la tele todo el día.

4. Oswaldo comió en su cuarto, pero sus amigos comieron en un restaurante famoso.

5. Oswaldo se quedó el hotel todo el día, pero sus amigos se quedaron en el centro hasta la medianoche.

6-3 Por última vez.

Answers will vary. The verb forms in the questions are:

1. invitó **2.** llevaron **3.** acampaste **4.** viajaste

6-4 ¿Qué tal las vacaciones?

1. pasé	**7.** Visitaron	**13.** sacó
2. gustó	**8.** pasaron	**14.** compré
3. viajaste	**9.** fuimos	**15.** regresaron/llegaron
4. acompañó	**10.** vimos	**16.** llegaron/regresaron
5. fue	**11.** Sacaste	**17.** llegamos
6. fue	**12.** Leí	**18.** descansé

6-6 ¿Adónde fueron?

1. a Sudamérica	**3.** al río	**5.** a varios restaurantes	**7.** al mercado
2. al mar	**4.** a un sitio histórico	**6.** al museo	**8.** al bosque

6-7 ¿Qué hicieron?

1. pasó
2. agradables
3. Visitó
4. abuelos
5. fue
6. gustaron
7. pasó
8. aburridas
9. fueron
10. llovió
11. se quedó
12. la tele y (muchos) vídeos

Tema 2 ¿Qué tal el vuelo?

6-8 Un vuelo.

Antes de despegar

Llegó al aeropuerto dos horas antes del vuelo.

Facturó su equipaje.

Fue a la sala de espera.

Esperó una hora y media.

Subió al avión.

Se abrochó el cinturón de seguridad.

Durante el vuelo

(The following four items may be in any order.)

Leyó la revista de la aerolínea.

Habló con el pasajero al lado de ella.

Vio toda la ciudad por la ventanilla.

Almorzó en el avión.

Después de aterrizar

Bajó del avión.

Recogió su equipaje.

Salió del aeropuerto.

Buscó un taxi.

Subió al taxi.

Fue a su hotel.

6-9 ¿En qué orden?

1. El avión despegó a las ocho de la mañana y aterrizó a las cuatro de la tarde.
2. El pasajero a mi lado sacó un libro y leyó durante todo el vuelo.
3. Saqué los audífonos y oí música.
4. Llegué a mi destino, bajé del avión y abracé a mi amiga que me recogió en el aeropuerto.

6-10 Dos viajes.

1. **Ella buscó** un hotel después de llegar pero **yo busqué** un hotel por Internet antes de salir.
2. **Ella pagó** mucho por su pasaje de avión porque esperó hasta el último momento para comprarlo, pero **yo pagué** muy poco porque compré el mío con dos meses de antelación.
3. **Yo llegué** muy bien a mi destino pero **ella llegó** muy cansada.
4. **Yo leí** mi guía para hacer un itinerario antes de salir pero **ella** nunca **leyó** su guía.
5. **Ella sacó** fotos con una cámara desechable porque dejó su cámara en casa, pero **yo saqué** fotos con mi nueva cámara digital que compré para el viaje.

6-11 La última lección de español.

Answers will vary. The verb forms in the questions are:

1. Llegaste   **2.** Oyeron   **3.** Leyeron   **4.** Almorzaste   **5.** Empezaste   **6.** Buscaste

6-13 Un vuelo.

1. El avión salió a tiempo.

2. Tomé un vuelo directo.

3. Almorcé antes de salir.

4. Sólo llevé una maleta pequeña.

5. Me senté junto al pasillo.

6. Me senté al fondo del avión.

7. Un pasajero aburrido me habló todo el tiempo.

8. Un amigo me recogió.

6-14 Un mal vuelo.

1. El vuelo **salió** a tiempo.

2. Veinte minutos después de despegar, los pasajeros **oyeron** algo en uno de los motores y algunos **vieron** fuego.

3. El avión empezó a volver al aeropuerto de donde **salió**.

4. Una pasajera a la derecha de Diego **empezó** a llorar, otra a su izquierda **leyó** tranquilamente y Diego **rezó** un poco.

5. El avión **llegó** al aeropuerto y **aterrizó** sin problema.

6. Diego **esperó** otro vuelo más tarde y por eso **llegó** con retraso.

Tema 3 ¿Te gustó el hotel?

6-15 En el hotel.

1. recepcionista	**4.** huésped	**7.** botones	**10.** mar	**13.** suelo / piso
2. pasillo	**5.** escalera	**8.** equipaje	**11.** balcón	**14.** baño
3. recepcionista	**6.** ascensor	**9.** llave	**12.** cama (matrimonial)	**15.** ducha

6-16 El fin de semana pasado.

1. Sus compañeros de casa se vistieron con ropa elegante para salir.

2. Felipe limpió la casa.

3. Sus compañeros de casa fueron a muchas fiestas.

4. Felipe jugó con los videojuegos en casa.

5. Sus compañeros de casa se divirtieron con los amigos.

6. Felipe se acostó temprano el sábado.

7. Felipe durmió mucho.

8. Sus compañeros de casa no volvieron a casa el sábado.

9. Sus compañeros de casa se despertaron muy cansados el lunes.

6-17 ¡Yo también!

Answers will vary.

6-18 Un día cargado.

1. Se acostó a las tres y **se despertó** a las siete.

2. Se bañó, se vistió y **salió** para el trabajo.

3. Llegó tarde a la oficina porque **perdió** el autobús.

4. Después de llegar, **se sirvió** un café, **se sentó** en su escritorio y **empezó** a trabajar.

5. A mediodía **almorzó** en un restaurante cerca de su oficina donde **probó** un plato nuevo.

6. Después de almorzar, **volvió** al trabajo donde **se quedó** hasta las cuatro.

6-20 Una habitación de hotel.

1. Hay dos habitaciones **disponibles** en el hotel.

2. Hay una habitación de **fumadores** en el **quinto** piso y otra de no **fumadores** en el **tercer** piso.

3. La habitación doble cuesta **750** pesos la noche y la habitación **sencilla** cuesta **580** pesos la noche.

4. La turista prefiere la habitación más **cara** porque prefiere una habitación de **no fumadores**.

6-21 ¿Por qué?

1. se despertó tarde	**6.** probó un plato de la región
2. se acostó muy tarde anoche	**7.** prefirió ir de compras
3. se divirtió toda la noche	**8.** no cambió dinero
4. almorzó en el hotel	**9.** no encontró un banco
5. pidió algo que no le gustó	**10.** perdió todas sus tarjetas de crédito

Tema 4 ¿Qué tal la habitación?

6-22 En el hotel.

1. Me desperté	**4.** me levanté	**7.** fui	**10.** champú	**13.** camarera	**16.** volvió	**19.** sábanas
2. oí	**5.** Puse	**8.** toallas	**11.** Me senté	**14.** trajo	**17.** hizo	**20.** dejó
3. despertador	**6.** calefacción	**9.** pedí	**12.** vi	**15.** me vestí	**18.** puso	**21.** papel higiénico

6-23 ¿Qué tiempo hizo?

1. En Ecuador todos **nos pusimos** camiseta y sandalias porque **hizo sol** todos los días. No **estuvo nublado** ni un sólo día.

2. En Buenos Aires **tuvimos** que comprar paraguas porque nadie **trajo** uno y **llovió** todo el tiempo.

3. En Chile **pudimos** esquiar porque **nevó** mucho justo antes de nuestra llegada.

6-24 Un viaje de negocios.

1. salió	**4.** fue	**7.** dijeron	**10.** repitió
2. llegó a	**5.** descansó	**8.** volvió	**11.** estuvo
3. se alojó	**6.** cenó	**9.** se acostó	**12.** se fue
			13. pudo

6-25 ¿Y tú? *The answers to the questions will vary. The verb forms in the questions are:*

1. hiciste   **2.** fuiste   **3.** estuviste   **4.** tuviste, pudiste   **5.** hizo   **6.** te pusiste   **7.** Trajiste

6-27 ¿No funciona o no hay?

1. no funciona   **3.** no hay   **5.** no funciona   **7.** no funciona

2. no hay   **4.** no funciona   **6.** no hay   **8.** no hay

6-28 Con los vecinos.

1. Ella hizo mucha comida.   **4.** Nadie hizo mucho.   **7.** Ella se puso el pijama.

2. Sus vecinos trajeron un pastel.   **5.** Sus vecinos estuvieron en la casa hasta las nueve.

3. Ella puso un CD.   **6.** Sus vecinos tuvieron que ir al aeropuerto.

6-29 Preguntas.

Answers will vary.

Tema 5 ¿Conoce usted bien la ciudad?

6-30 Unos mandados.

1. Hizo una llamada internacional en un teléfono público.

2. Durmió hasta tarde en el hotel.

3. Se cortó el pelo en la peluquería.

4. Mandó unas tarjetas postales en la oficina de correos.

5. Probó un plato típico de la región en el restaurante del hotel.

6. Cambió unos cheques de viaje en el banco.

7. Pidió medicamentos para las alergias en la farmacia.

8. Pudo encontrar información sobre las excursiones en la región en la agencia de viajes.

9. Visitó una exposición en el museo.

10. Vio una obra en el teatro.

11. Compró gasolina en la gasolinera.

6-31 En la recepción.

1. conozco   **2.** Sabe   **3.** Conoce   **4.** sé   **5.** conozco   **6.** sé

6-32 En mi familia.

Answers will vary.

6-33 ¿Saber o conocer?

The answers to the questions will vary. The verb forms in the questions are:

1. sabes   **2.** Conoces   **3.** Sabes   **4.** Conoces   **5.** Sabes

6-35 Dificultades.

1. una peluquería

2. una oficina de correos

3. una farmacia abierta

4. un banco abierto

5. un teléfono público

6-36 ¿Me podría decir...?

1. El turista busca una **librería** para comprar una **guía turística**.

2. Para llegar al lugar que busca, debe ir a la **derecha** al **salir** del hotel. Necesita **seguir recto** tres **cuadras**.

3. El turista también quiere comprar un **periódico internacional**.

4. Si no lo tienen en el primer lugar, el turista puede comprarlo en un **quiosco** a una **cuadra** del hotel a la **izquierda**.

6-37 En el taxi.

1. El taxista conoce **la calle Once.**

2. El taxista no conoce **el restaurante (La Terraza).**

3. El taxista sabe dónde **está la calle San Francisco.**

4. El taxista no sabe cuánto **tiempo va a llevar llegar al restaurante.**

Capítulo 7

Tema 1 ¿Cómo eras de niño/a?

7-1 Profesiones.

1. un maestro
2. unos obreros de fábrica
3. un policía
4. un médico
5. una secretaria
6. una programadora
7. un hombre de negocios
8. unos actores
9. unos jugadores de fútbol
10. unos músicos

7-2 ¿A qué se dedican?

1. Una actriz se dedica a hacer teatro.
2. Los maestros se dedican a enseñar a los niños.
3. Un deportista se dedica a practicar deportes.
4. Los obreros de la construcción se dedican a construir casas.
5. Un enfermero se dedica a ayudar a los enfermos.
6. Un músico se dedica a hacer música.

7-3 Las montañas.

1. tenía
2. vivía
3. tenía
4. hablaba
5. tocaba
6. escuchaba
7. veíamos
8. gustaba
9. leía
10. jugaban
11. hacían
12. paseaban
13. hablaban
14. pasaba

7-4 ¡Qué cambio!

1. Cuando era niña, a Soledad no le gustaba pasar tiempo sola porque siempre quería jugar con alguien.
2. Cuando era niña, Soledad siempre iba a misa los domingos porque era muy religiosa.
3. Cuando era niña, Soledad no era muy tímida con las personas que no conocía porque era muy curiosa sobre todos.
4. Cuando era niña, Soledad tenía mucho tiempo libre porque no tenía mucha tarea para la escuela.
5. Cuando era niña, había muchos niños en el vecindario porque vivía en un vecindario con muchas familias.

7-6 La familia de Jorge.

1. maestro
2. actriz
3. programador
4. artistas
5. obrero de la construcción
6. profesora

7-7 De niño y ahora.

1. de niño
2. de niño
3. de niño
4. ahora
5. de niño
6. de niño
7. de niño
8. ahora
9. ahora

Answers to the second part will vary.

Tema 2 Los grandes acontecimientos de la vida

7-8 Acontecimientos.

1. nacimiento 3. cumpleaños 5. licencia de manejar 7. graduación
2. boda 4. funeral 6. jubilación 8. concurso

7-9 ¿Qué pasó?

1. b **2.** e **3.** f **4.** c **5.** d **6.** a

Answers to the second part will vary.

7-10 El día de su graduación.

1. Toda mi familia **fue** a su graduación y mis padres **estaban** muy orgullosos.

2. El día de la graduación **llovía** y **hacía** muy mal tiempo cuando **llegamos**.

3. Mi hemano **se puso** la toga mientras **esperábamos** el comienzo de la ceremonia.

4. Mis padres **sacaron** muchas fotos de mi hermano porque **estaba** muy guapo en la toga.

5. Mi hermano nos **vio** cuando **entró** con los otros estudiantes porque **estábamos** cerca de la entrada.

6. Mis padres y yo **conocimos** a la novia de mi hermano mientras **celebrábamos** la fiesta de Eduardo.

7. Mi hermano y ella **se abrazaban** cuando mis padres y yo los **vimos**.

7-11 ¡Qué triste!

1. nos despertamos 4. perdió 7. bebían
2. nevaba 5. empezó 8. manejamos
3. esperaban 6. se sintió 9. se celebró

7-13 ¿Qué acontecimiento? 1. la boda 3. el funeral 5. la jubilación 7. la licencia de manejar

2. la graduación 4. el campeonato 6. la quinceañera 8. el nacimiento

7-14 ¡Qué buenos recuerdos!

1. ganó 2. marqué 3. conocí 4. estábamos 5. se fue 6. se casó

Tema 3 Mis cuentos preferidos

7-15 Mi cuento favorito.

1. gustaba 3. era 5. se arrepintió 7. volvió
2. contaba 4. ahogó 6. encontraron 8. oían

7-16 La Malinche.

1. nació	5. era	9. dijeron	13. vivió	17. supo	21. era
2. era	6. volvió	10. estaba	14. llegó	18. sabía	22. dijo
3. se llamaba	7. tuvo	11. celebraron	15. ofrecieron	19. conocía	23. fue
4. murió	8. vendieron	12. vendieron	16. pusieron	20. entendió	

7-17 Cortés y Marina.

1. aprendió	5. ofrecía	9. convocaron	13. iban	17. abrazó	21. perdió
2. hizo	6. vencieron	10. vinieron	14. vio	18. salió	22. Entregó
3. sentía	7. llamaban	11. estaba	15. lloraban	19. fue	
4. traducía	8. tuvo	12. creían	16. consoló	20. murieron	

7-18 El día de Analissa.

Por la mañana

1. Cuando sonó el despertador, Analissa tenía mucho sueño y durmió un poco más.

2. No tuvo/tenía tiempo para desayunar y compró un café en la calle.

3. Hacía buen tiempo y decidió caminar a la oficina.

4. Cuando llegó a la oficina, su jefe estaba esperándola.

Por la tarde

5. Salió a almorzar con Paquita pero la comida en el restaurante era muy mala.

6. Había mucho que hacer en la oficina y trabajó toda la tarde sin descanso.

7. No tenía mucha energía y se sentía muy cansada.

8. No pudo terminar el trabajo y se lo llevó a casa.

Por la noche

9. Asistió a una fiesta de jubilación de un compañero.

10. Después de la fiesta, volvió a casa. Estaba muy cansada.

11. Quería ver una película, pero no había nada bueno en la televisión.

12. Se acostó temprano y se durmió pronto.

7-20 Mi boda.

1. Ana vivía en Florida y estudiaba economía en la universidad.

2. Durante la semana asistía a sus clases y pasaba mucho tiempo en la biblioteca. Los fines de semana trabajaba en un restaurante muy elegante en la playa.

3. Laura tenía un amigo chef, Rubén, y lo llamó para pedirle ayuda.

4. Ana conoció a su futuro esposo.

5. Rubén y Ana fueron novios por un año y medio.

6. Se casaron en San Juan de Puerto Rico en febrero del año 2002.

7. Su boda fue muy, muy divertida. Tuvieron una ceremonia religiosa y un gran banquete con muchos invitados.

7-21 ¿Qué heroína?

1. Pocahontas   **2.** La Guanina   **3.** La Cenicienta   **4.** La Llorona

Tema 4 ¿Cómo era el vecindario?

7-22 El centro de la ciudad.

1. un policía	5. un semáforo	9. un taller	13. una parada de autobús
2. un peatón	6. el límite de velocidad	10. un letrero	14. una acera
3. el tráfico/la circulación	7. la autopista	11. una esquina	15. una grúa
4. un edificio	8. un estacionamiento	12. una multa	16. un/a conductor/a

7-23 ¿Qué se hace?

1. se espera el autobús	3. se maneja rápido	5. se respira aire contaminado
2. se arreglan autos	4. se conoce a todos los vecinos	6. se guardan los carros

7-24 Antes y hoy.

1. Antes se jugaba mucho en la calle y hoy se mira demasiado la televisión.

2. Antes se vivía más tranquilo en la ciudad y hoy se necesita tener cuidado con el tráfico.

3. Antes se podía andar mucho a pie y hoy se maneja más.

4. Antes se veían más espacios verdes y hoy se hacen autopistas grandes.

5. Antes se veían menos accidentes en las calles y hoy se encuentran choques de autos todos los días.

7-25 Hace cincuenta años.

1. Sí, se respiraba aire más fresco.   **4.** No, no se ponían muchas multas.

2. No, no se pasaban muchas horas en el tráfico.   **5.** Sí, se vivía mejor. / No, no se vivía mejor.

3. Sí, se preparaba la comida en la casa.

7-27 Buenos Aires

1. Falso. La presencia de la inmigración europea es evidente en muchos rincones de Buenos Aires.

2. Cierto

3. Falso. Todavía hoy las Madres de la Plaza de Mayo marchan cada jueves en protesta por sus hijos desaparecidos.

4. Cierto

5. Falso. En el barrio de La Boca se establecieron inmigrantes italianos.

6. Cierto

7-28 ¿Qué es apropiado?

1. No, en las autopistas se maneja a alta velocidad.   **4.** No, se espera el autobús en la parada del autobús.

2. No, los autos se dejan en un estacionamiento.   **5.** No, se dan multas a los conductores.

3. No, se anda a pie por la acera.   **6.** No, se respira aire contaminado.

Tema 5 ¿Vio usted lo que pasó?

7-29 ¿Qué hacer?

1. emergencia 4. víctimas 7. ambulancia
2. chocar 5. paramédicos 8. bomberos
3. policía 6. primeros auxilios 9. heridos

7-30 Un robo.

1. viniste 2. fui 3. ocurrió 4. volvía 5. asaltó 6. vino 7. hubo 8. vio

7-31 El informe del accidente.

1. iba 2. giró 3. venía 4. pudo 5. chocaron 6. resultó 7. hubo 8. estaban 9. llegó

7-32 ¿Cómo ocurrió?

1. hacía, chocaron

Hablaba por teléfono, tomaba (una) cerveza, escuchaba música.

2. estaba, estaba

Estaba sola.

3. paró, Manejaba

No paró porque miraba a un muchacho en la calle y no vio la luz roja. Sí, manejaba rápido.

4. Resultó

No, pero un hombre cruzando la calle casi resultó herido.

5. Había, Vieron

Sí, había más gente en la calle. Sí, vieron el accidente.

7-34 911, ¿en qué puedo ayudarle?

1. emergencia 3. herido 5. opuesta 7. testigos 9. semáforo
2. chocar 4. ocurrió 6. ambulancia 8. cruzar 10. resultó

7-35 El incendio.

1. cerré, salí 2. salía 3. supe, llamó 4. resultó 5. pagué 6. pude

Capítulo 8 En el restaurante

Tema 1 ¿Qué me recomienda?

8-1 En la mesa.

a. una botella   **c.** una copa   **e.** una taza   **g.** un tenedor   **i.** un plato llano   **k.** una cuchara

b. un vaso   **d.** un mantel   **f.** una servilleta   **h.** un plato hondo   **j.** un cuchillo

8-2 ¿Para qué se usa?

1. b, c   **2.** h, k   **3.** e   **4.** a, c   **5.** d   **6.** f

8-3 Me das…

1. ¿Me das un vaso de limonada, por favor?   **3.** ¿Me das una botella de cerveza, por favor?

2. ¿Me das una copa de vino tinto, por favor?   **4.** ¿Me das una taza de café, por favor?

8-4 En el restaurante.

1. la terraza   **2.** la propina   **3.** el menú   **4.** la carta de vinos   **5.** la caja   **6.** la cuenta   **7.** el carrito de postres

8-5 ¿Qué hacían?

1. Arturo le proponía matrimonio a Mónica.

2. Mónica le contestaba que sí a Arturo.

3. Javier le daba la cuenta a la cajera.

4. Orlando, Fernanda y Juan le pedían la comida a la mesera.

5. La mesera les describía el plato del día a Orlando, Fernanda y Juan.

6. El mesero les ofrecía postres a Blanca y Jazmín.

7. Carlos e Isabel le dejaban una propina al mesero (a la mesera).

8-6 ¡Qué buen servicio!

1. Yo **le pregunté** qué prefería él y **me recomendó** la paella.

2. El mesero **me preguntó** si podía retirar mi plato sucio y **le contesté** que sí.

3. Mi amigo **le pidió** un trozo de pastel al mesero, pero yo **le dije** que no quería postre.

4. El mesero **me dio** la cuenta a mí, pero yo **le dije** que mi amigo iba a pagar.

5. El mesero **nos dio** muy buen servicio, entonces nosotros **le dejamos** una buena propina.

8-8 En el restaurante.

a. 3   **b.** 5   **c.** 6   **d.** 1   **e. Modelo**   **f.** 2   **g.** 7   **h.** 8   **i.** 9   **j.** 4

1. el mesero   **4.** el mesero   **7.** el mesero

2. el cliente   **5.** el mesero   **8.** el cliente

3. el mesero   **6.** el cliente   **9.** el cliente

8-9 ¿Y tú?

Answers will vary.

Tema 2 ¿Qué desea usted?

8-10 ¿Qué se le pone?

1. Le pongo mantequilla al pan tostado.

2. Les pongo azúcar a los cereales.

3. Le pongo azúcar al café.

4. Les pongo sal a los huevos.

5. Les pongo sal (y mantequilla) a las zanahorias.

6. Le pongo sal al pescado.

8-11 Preferencias.

1. ¿Prefieres **el café** con crema, con azúcar o solo?

   Me gusta más solo (con crema, con azúcar, con crema y azúcar). / No me gusta el café.

2. ¿Prefieres **la ensalada** con lechuga o espinacas? ¿con muchos tomates? ¿con o sin cebolla?

   Me gusta más con lechuga (con espinacas). Me gusta con muchos tomates. (No me gusta con muchos tomates. / Me gusta sin tomates.) Me gusta con (sin) cebolla. / No me gusta la ensalada.

3. ¿Prefieres **los camarones** fritos o a la parrilla?

   Me gustan más fritos (a la parrilla). / No me gustan los camarones.

4. ¿Prefieres **el té** helado o caliente?

   Me gusta más helado (caliente). / No me gusta el té.

5. ¿Prefieres **el pan tostado** con mantequilla o con mermelada?

   Me gusta más sin nada (con mantequilla pero sin mermelada, con mantequilla y mermelada, con mermelada pero sin mantequilla). / No me gusta el pan tostado.

6. ¿Prefieres **los huevos** fritos o revueltos?

   Me gustan más fritos (revueltos). / No me gustan los huevos.

7. ¿Prefieres **las zanahorias** cocidas o crudas?

   Me gustan más cocidas (crudas). / No me gustan las zanahorias.

8-12 ¿Qué le gusta?

1. Le encanta la ensalada.

2. Le gusta el helado.

3. Le da asco el jamón.

4. Le dan asco los camarones.

5. Le encantan los espárragos.

6. Le encanta el arroz.

7. Le gusta el pastel (de chocolate).

8. Le dan asco las chuletas de cerdo.

9. Le encantan las papas fritas.

8-13 Marco y Cristina.

1. A Cristina le molesta mucho el humo en la sección de fumadores.

2. A Marco no le importa el precio de un restaurante.

3. A Marco le duele el estómago a veces porque come mucha grasa.

4. A Cristina le dan asco los platos con mucha grasa.

5. A Marco no le interesa comer platos sanos.

6. A Marco le encantan los postres.

8-15 Orden de preferencia.

1. — el pollo
2. — el jamón
3. — el pescado
4. — las chuletas de cerdo
5. — el bistec
6. — los camarones

8-16 Un mal restaurante.

1. A él no le gusta **el bistec** que le sirvieron porque contiene **mucha grasa** y no está **bien cocido** como lo pidió.

2. Normalmente, a ella le **encanta la sopa de cebolla** pero no puede tomar la que le sirvieron esta noche. Le falta **cebolla** y es como **agua** con **sal**.

3. Parece que al mesero le molesta **venir (ir) a la mesa** de los clientes.

4. Al cliente le falta **un cuchillo** para **cortar la carne**.

5. Al mesero no le importa **servir a los clientes**. Le interesa más **hablar con la otra mesera**.

6. Parece que al mesero no le interesa **su (la) propina**.

7. A la clienta le molesta **pagar la cuenta**.

8-17 ¿Y tú?

Answers will vary.

Tema 3 En el mercado

8-18 Un puesto en el mercado.

1. las naranjas
2. los plátanos
3. las piñas
4. los melones
5. las manzanas
6. las uvas
7. las papas
8. el brócoli
9. la lechuga
10. los espárragos
11. las zanahorias
12. las cebollas

8-19 ¿A qué se lo pongo?

1. Se las voy a poner a la ensalada de fruta.
2. Se las voy a poner a la ensalada de espinacas.
3. Se la voy a poner al café.
4. Se lo voy a poner a la ensalada de espinacas.
5. Se los voy a poner a la ensalada de espinacas.
6. Se las voy a poner a la ensalada de fruta.

8-20 ¿A quién?

1. Se lo puedo servir a él, pero a ella no.
2. Se lo puedo servir a ella, pero a él no.
3. Se las puedo servir a ella, pero a él no.
4. Se las puedo servir a los dos.
5. Se los puedo servir a los dos.
6. Se lo puedo servir a ella, pero a él no.

8-21 Una fiesta.

1. Daniel se la describía.
2. Francisco se las traía.
3. Se la ofrecía a Roberto.
4. Nadie se la daba.
5. Se los contaba a Julia, Enrique y Guadalupe
6. Se lo iba a dar a María.

8-22 ¿Quién?

1. El mesero me recomendó el plato del día y yo se lo pedí.

2. Yo le hice preguntas sobre el menú y él me lo explicó.

3. Él me ofrecio un postre pero yo le dije que no quería nada más.

4. Yo le pedí la cuenta y él me la trajo.

5. Yo le di una tarjeta de crédito y el me la devolvió.

8-24 ¿Qué hay en la nevera?

In the refrigerator there should be an X next to the: fish, lettuce, tomatoes, onions, apples, bread, eggs, orange juice, milk, coffee.

A comprar: camarones, arroz, brócoli, naranjas, plátanos, fresas, agua mineral, vino blanco, jamón.

8-25 Respuestas.

1. Sí, nos lo dieron.

2. Sí, se los recomiendo.

3. Sí, voy a traérsela ahora.

4. No, mi amigo se lo pidió.

5. Sí, ¿nos la trae, por favor?

6. Sí, me la acaba de traer.

Tema 4 Una receta

8-26 Indicaciones.

1. Caliente el jamón.

2. Agréguele sal y pimienta a la sopa.

3. Bata los huevos.

4. Mezcle la ensalada.

8-27 Una sopa de verduras.

1. Sí, agréguelos.

2. No, no la agregue.

3. Sí, agréguelas.

4. No, no las agregue.

5. Sí, agréguelo.

6. No, no lo agregue.

8-28 Consejos.

1. Desayunen todas las mañanas. No cenen muy tarde.

2. No fumen. Dejen de fumar.

3. Duerman lo suficiente. No se acuesten muy tarde.

4. No tomen mucha cerveza. Eviten el alcohol.

5. No coman mucha carne roja. Pidan pescado o pollo.

6. No salgan todos los días a restaurantes. Preparen comida sana en casa.

7. Hagan ejercicio con regularidad. No sean perezosos.

8. Vayan al médico si están enfermos. No vengan a clase enfermos.

8-29 Consejos.

Rankings in the right column will vary.

1. Dedique (Ud.)

2. No dedique (Ud.)

3. No sea (Ud.)

4. No insista (Ud.)

5. Siga (Ud.)

6. No se acueste (Ud.)

7. No pierda (Ud.)

8. Tenga (Ud.)

9. No piense (Ud.)

10. Diviértase (Ud.)

11. Organice (Ud.)

12. Tenga (Ud.)

13. No haga (Ud.)

14. Vaya (Ud.)

8-30 Cortesía.

1. Sí, ¿me explica qué hay en el mole, por favor?

2. ¿Me lo prepara término medio, por favor?

3. ¿Me da el brócoli y las espinacas, por favor?

4. ¿Me la sirve ahora, por favor?

5. ¿Me trae la cuenta, por favor?

8-32 Receta de galletas de choco-chip.

Ingredientes:

1 **taza de mantequilla** derretida

1 **cucharada de vainilla**

3/4 de **taza de azúcar** blanco

2 **huevos**

1/2 de **taza de azúcar** moreno

1-1/2 taza de confi-chips de **chocolate**

2-1/4 **tazas de harina**

1 cucharadita de polvo de hornear

1/2 cucharadita de **sal**

Preparación:

1. En **un recipiente, bata** la mantequilla, los azúcares, la vainilla y los huevos.

2. Agregue la harina, el polvo de hornear y **la sal.**

3. Mezcle hasta formar una pasta.

4. Agregue los confi-chips de **chocolate.**

5. Forme bolitas aplastadas y **póngalas** en una charola de horno engrasada y enharinada.

6. Precaliente el horno a 190°C.

7. Deje las galletas en el horno de ocho a diez minutos.

8-33 El señor o la señora Modales.

1. Sí, sírvaselo frío (a los invitados).

2. Póngalos a la izquierda del plato.

3. Sírvaselo (a los invitados) en un plato limpio.

4. Sí, retírelos (de la mesa) antes de servir el postre.

Tema 5 Una dieta

8-34 ¿Me los recomiendas?

1. No, no te lo recomiendo porque contiene **mucha grasa.**

2. Sí, te las recomiendo porque contienen **mucha vitamina A.**

3. No, no te lo recomiendo porque contiene **mucha cafeína.**

4. Sí, te las recomiendo porque contienen **varias vitaminas.**

5. No, no te los recomiendo porque contienen **mucho azúcar.**

6. Sí, te los recomiendo porque contienen **mucha fibra.**

8-35 Repite, por favor.

1. **No lo comas** con frecuencia porque contiene **mucha grasa.**

2. **Cómelas** con frecuencia porque contienen **mucha vitamina A.**

3. **No lo tomes** con frecuencia porque contiene **mucha cafeína.**

4. **Cómelas** con frecuencia porque contienen **varias vitaminas.**

5. **No los tomes** con frecuencia porque contienen **mucho azúcar.**

6. **Cómelos** con frecuencia porque contienen **mucha fibra.**

8-36 Mandatos.

Tú Affirmative	Tú Negative	Ud. All Commands	Uds. All Commands
1. deja	no dejes	(no) deje	(no) dejen
2. evita	no evites	(no) evite	(no) eviten
3. toma	no tomes	(no) tome	(no) tomen
4. empieza	no empieces	(no) empiece	(no) empiecen
5. come	no comas	(no) coma	(no) coman
6. pierde	no pierdas	(no) pierda	(no) pierdan
7. sé	no seas	(no) sea	(no) sean
8. haz	no hagas	(no) haga	(no) hagan
9. ve	no vayas	(no) vaya	(no) vayan
10. sal	no salgas	(no) salga	(no) salgan

1. Empiecen el día con ejercicio.

2. No seas perezoso/a.

3. Haz ejercicio conmigo.

4. Eviten el alcohol y la cafeína.

5. No pierdan la paciencia.

6. Ve al gimnasio conmigo.

8-37 Consejos.

1. Pues, **¡sal más temprano de casa!**

2. Pues, **¡ponte un suéter!**

3. Pues, **¡trae algo para comer entre las clases!**

4. Pues, **¡ve a ver al profesor a su oficina!**

5. Sí, cómo no, **¡ven conmigo a la biblioteca!**

8-39 Tú también.

1. Tú también, Benjamín, evita los dulces.

2. Tú también, Benjamín, ten una dieta equilibrada.

3. Tú también, Benjamín, haz ejercicio todos los días.

4. Tú también, Benjamín, sé menos impaciente.

5. Tú también, Benjamín, ponte crema protectora.

6. Tú también, Benjamín, acuéstate más temprano.

7. Tú también, Benjamín, lávate los dientes antes de acostarte.

8-40 Recomendaciones.

1. **Ven** al gimnasio conmigo.

2. **No vayas** a los bufetes.

3. **Evita** los platos con mucha grasa.

4. **Acuéstate** un rato.

5. **No salgas** con ellos.

Capítulo 9

Tema 1 ¿Te lastimaste?

9-1 El cuerpo.

1. el cabello	4. el corazón	7. el pie	10. la cara	13. la mano	16. la pierna
2. el ojo	5. el brazo	8. la cabeza	11. la boca	14. los dedos	17. el tobillo
3. el diente	6. la rodilla	9. la nariz	12. el pecho	15. el estómago	

9-2 ¡Cuidado!

1. Ten cuidado. No te caigas de la escalera.

2. No te pongas nerviosa por el examen. Relájate.

3. No te resfríes. Ponte un suéter.

4. No te quemes la espalda con el sol. Ponte crema protectora.

5. Levántate con cuidado. No te des un golpe contra la mesa.

6. Ponte zapatos buenos. No te tuerzas el tobillo durante la carrera.

9-3 ¡Cuídense!

1. ¡No corras tan rápido con el caballo! ¡Te vas a caer y romper la pierna!

2. ¡No sean tan impacientes con la comida! ¡Se van a quemar la boca!

3. ¡No juegues cerca de la mesa! ¡Te vas a lastimar (dar un golpe en) la cabeza!

4. ¡Pónganse crema protectora solar! ¡Se van a quemar la piel!

5. ¡No uses zapatos de tacón tan alto! ¡Te vas a torcer el tobillo!

6. ¡Ten más cuidado con el cuchillo! ¡Te vas a cortar el dedo!

9-4 ¿Te duele mucho?

1. pasó	3. me caí	5. enyesada	7. duele	9. quitar
2. te lastimaste	4. vendado	6. duele	8. muletas	10. me resfrié

9-6 ¿Qué te pasó?

1. Te lastimaste	3. me caí	5. me torcí	7. me di	9. deprimida
2. montaba	4. Te rompiste	6. te duele	8. quitan	10. Ya no

9-7 Advertencias.

1. Beatriz, te vas a lastimar **la pierna**. **¡No te lastimes la pierna!**

2. Juan, Carlos, se van a poner malos del **estómago**. **¡No se pongan malos del estómago!**

3. Julia, te vas a quemar **la mano**. **¡No te quemes la mano!**

4. Sara, Pedro, se van a torcer **el tobillo**. **¡No se tuerzan el tobillo!**

5. Enrique, te vas a dar un golpe en **la cabeza**. **¡No te des un golpe en la cabeza!**

6. Lola, Carla, se van a caer de **espalda**. **¡No se caigan de espalda!**

Tema 2 ¡Cuídense!

9-8 En la clase de salud.

1. cuidar	**3.** alimentos	**5.** atún	**7.** vitaminas	**9.** estirarse
2. mantenerse	**4.** ejercicio	**6.** ricos	**8.** sistema inmunológico	**10.** prevenir

9-9 A dieta.

1. Vamos al gimnasio cada mañana a las siete.

2. Sigamos una dieta sana y equilibrada para bajar de peso.

3. Desayunemos fuerte y cenemos ligero.

4. Hagamos platos bajos en calorías.

5. No les pongamos mucha sal a las comidas.

6. Tengamos cuidado con los productos ricos en grasa.

7. No durmamos todo el tiempo.

8. Demos un paseo después de cada comida.

9-10 Estados y resultados.

1. Durmamos una siesta.

2. Pongámonos crema protectora.

3. Tomemos un agua mineral.

4. Pidamos una ensalada de fruta.

5. Vamos en bicicleta.

9-11 Una dieta equilibrada.

1. No tomemos demasiada cerveza.

2. Comamos pescado.

3. Evitemos usar demasiada mantequilla.

4. Preparemos zanahorias.

5. No hagamos un pastel.

6. Sirvamos fresas.

9-12 ¿Y tú?

Answers will vary.

9-14 En la clínica *A la medida.*

1. pesado	**3.** ayudar	**5.** se encuentran	**7.** equilibrada	**9.** cuidar
2. fatiga	**4.** bajar de peso	**6.** dieta	**8.** mantener	**10.** manos

9-15 Una vida sana.

1. Hagamos una ensalada.

2. No le pongamos mucho azúcar al té.

3. Comamos fruta de postre.

4. No, no le agreguemos más sal a la sopa.

5. Hagamos ejercicio antes de comer.

6. Cenemos ligero.

7. Evitemos la cafeína.

8. Desayunemos antes de salir mañana.

9. Sigamos nuestra dieta.\

10. Compremos productos frescos.

Tema 3 ¿Qué síntomas tiene?

9-16 ¿Qué les duele?

1. Estornuda.	**3.** Le duele el oído.	**5.** Le pican los ojos.	**7.** Tiene el dedo hinchado.
2. Tiene catarro.	**4.** Tiene fiebre.	**6.** Se siente mareada.	**8.** Necesita una curita.

9-17 No me siento bien, doctor.

Answers will vary.

9-18 Recomendaciones.

1. guarde cama
2. coma comidas muy picantes
3. no hagan muchas actividades al aire libre
4. organicemos mejor nuestro tiempo
5. no juegues al fútbol por unas semanas
6. tomemos más vitaminas

9-19 Preferencias.

Some answers may vary.

1. coma mucha grasa
2. sean individuales
3. no tenga muchas visitas
4. ver a un médico
5. hagamos ejercicio
6. sentirse mejor pronto
7. fumen en las habitaciones
8. cuidar a los pacientes

9-21 ¿Qué síntomas tiene?

1. me siento mareada
2. vomito
3. tiene fiebre
4. guarde cama
5. Me duele el oído
6. toso mucho
7. examinarte la garganta
8. recetar
9. te pongas
10. Estornudo
11. me pican los ojos
12. alergia
13. unas pastillas
14. salga

9-22 ¿Se cuida?

Answers will vary.

Tema 4 ¿Quiere vivir 100 años?

9-23 Consejos para una vida más larga.

1. No trabajen más todo el tiempo.
2. Manejen con cuidado.
3. Vayan al médico una vez al año.
4. Tomen el sol con moderación.
5. No lleven una vida con estrés.
6. No suban de peso.
7. No consuman muchas bebidas alcohólicas.
8. Hagan ejercicio con regularidad.
9. Estírense antes de hacer ejercicio.
10. No tomen comidas con mucha sal.
11. Manténganse en contacto con la naturaleza.
12. Tengan siempre tiempo para relajarse.

9-24 En caso de infarto.

1. Prevenga   2. Tenga   3. abuse   4. se ponga   5. Insista   6. trate   7. Prohíba

9-25 Es una lástima…

1. más vale
2. vayas al médico
3. Ojalá
4. se sienta mejor pronto
5. Es preferible
6. vayas al médico
7. es común
8. se enferme
9. es normal
10. estés deprimido

9-26 Reacciones.

Answers will vary.

9-28 Consejos.

a. 4   **b.** 3   **c.** 1   **e.** 5   **f.** 2

9-29 Es bueno que…

1. mantengas una dieta rica

2. siempre te pongas crema protectora

3. te hagas

4. no fumes con regularidad

5. no tengas mucho estrés

6. manejes ebrio

Tema 5 La dieta y las enfermedades

9-30 Sufre de…

1. Sufro de congestión.   **2.** Sufren de artritis.   **3.** Sufre de fiebre del heno.   **4.** Sufre de diabetes.

9-31 Definiciones.

1. la sangre   **3.** los huesos   **5.** el cerebro   **7.** el estómago

2. el corazón   **4.** los pulmones   **6.** los riñones   **8.** el páncreas

1. los pulmones   **3.** el corazón   **5.** la sangre / el corazón   **7.** el estómago

2. el páncreas   **4.** los huesos   **6.** los riñones

9-32 Dudo que…

Answers will vary.

9-33 En la consulta.

1. Me siento   **4.** tos   **7.** recetar   **10.** sea   **13.** vuelva

2. síntomas   **5.** pulmones   **8.** alérgico   **11.** se cuide

3. garganta   **6.** grados   **9.** penicilina   **12.** guarde

9-34 Es posible que…

1. es posible que tengas alergia   **2.** es posible que estés deprimido   **3.** es posible que tengas gripe

9-36 ¿De qué sufren?

1. Es posible que sufra de insomnio.

2. Dudo que vaya al trabajo hoy.

3. Es posible que tenga diabetes.

4. Quizás sea un infarto.

5. Es probable que sufra de artritis.

6. Dudo que sea grave.

7. Quizás sufra de depresión.

8. Tal vez esté roto.

9-37 ¿Estás segura?

1. tiene pulmonía   **4.** guardar cama   **7.** descanse

2. tenga pulmonía   **5.** guarde cama   **8.** tengas razón

3. sea un catarro   **6.** se cuida mucho   **9.** escuche

Capítulo 10

Tema 1 En la oficina

10-1 En la oficina.

1. una (en)grapadora	**3.** un enchufe	**5.** un monitor	**7.** un teclado
2. una impresora	**4.** un calendario	**6.** un ratón	**8.** un archivador

10-2 ¿Cómo están?

1. Juan está desorganizado.

2. Juan y Beti están sentados.

3. Beti está relajada.

4. Beti está distraída.

5. Marco y Luz están enamorados.

6. El padre está enojado.

7. La madre está deprimida.

8. Luz está vestida de rebelde.

9. El hermanito y la madre están preocupados.

10-3 ¡Qué desorden!

1. desordenado	**3.** acostados	**5.** abierto	**7.** puesto	**9.** apagada	**11.** pintadas
2. dejada	**4.** hecha	**6.** cerrados	**8.** sentado	**10.** colgadas	

10-4 Mi cuarto.

Answers will vary.

10-5 Entrevista.

1. conocidas

2. escritos, recibidos

3. preferido, publicado

4. sorprendido/a, dichas, vistas

Answers to the questions will vary.

10-7 ¿Qué dice después?

1. _____ Todo está **preparado** para la reunión con los clientes.

   __X__ Los informes para la reunión no están **impresos**.

2. __X__ Todos los clientes están **sentados** y esperan **aburridos**.

   _____ Todos los clientes están muy **divertidos** porque el jefe es muy cómico y les está contando chistes.

3. __X__ El jefe se siente **perdido** si no tiene su presentación **escrita** con *Power Point*.

   _____ Al jefe no le gustan las presentaciones **hechas** con *Power Point*.

4. __X__ La computadora está **arreglada** y los informes están **terminados**.

   _____ Los problemas con los informes y la computadora todavía no están **resueltos**.

10-8 El primer día.

1. El amigo se ve muy **cansado**. Él se siente un poco **resfriado** y tiene los pulmones un poco **congestionados**.

2. Está **acostado** en el sofá porque tiene la espalda **lastimada**. Tuvo que mover unos muebles **pesados**.

3. Ahora la oficina está **ordenada** con la computadora **instalada** y la impresora **conectada**. Todo está **preparado** para mañana, ¡menos él!

Tema 2 Un currículum vitae

10-9 Mi currículum.

Answers will vary.

10-10 Búsqueda de trabajo.

1. a tiempo completo
2. a tiempo parcial
3. Además
4. empleo
5. aumento de sueldo
6. colegas
7. un jefe
8. gruñona
9. de mal humor
10. otros idiomas
11. a nivel alto
12. a nivel básico
13. la ubicación de
14. mudarme

10-11 ¿Hace cuánto tiempo?

1. Hace dos meses que mi novio cambió de trabajo. / Hace dos meses que tiene su nuevo trabajo.
2. Hace un año que mis vecinos se mudaron al lado. / Hace un año que viven aquí.
3. Hace medio año que mi hermana tiene un trabajo en diseño gráfico. /
   Hace medio año que se graduó de la universidad.
4. Hace un semestre que mi compañera de casa sacó la licenciatura. /
   Hace un semestre que hace estudios graduados.
5. Hace dos años que (yo) estudio en esta universidad. /
   Hace dos años que (yo) terminé la preparatoria.
6. Hace unos minutos que nosotros comenzamos este ejercicio. /
   Hace unos minutos que nosotros lo hacemos (lo estamos haciendo / estamos haciéndolo).

10-13 Con una asesora de empleo.

1. Hace tres meses que él **se graduó / tiene la licenciatura**.
2. Hace dos meses que **busca trabajo**.
3. En un trabajo, quiere sobre todo la oportunidad de ser creativo y **un buen salario**.
4. La oportunidad de ser creativo tiene más importancia porque no quiere estar **aburrido (en el trabajo)**.
5. **El ambiente de trabajo** es muy importante también porque quiere llevarse bien con sus **colegas**.
6. **La ubicación** no es vital porque no le importa **mudarse**.

10-14 ¿Cuándo?

1. Yezenia está enferma **desde hace cuatro días**. ¿Qué día **se enfermó**?
   Se enfermó el martes / el 13 de diciembre.
2. Yezenia **no va al trabajo** desde hace tres días. ¿Cuál **fue** su último día **en el trabajo**?
   Su último día en el trabajo fue el miércoles / el 14 de diciembre.
3. **Hace cuarenta y cinco minutos que** Yezenia está en la sala de espera del doctor. ¿A qué hora **llegó**?
   Llegó (a la oficina del doctor) a las diez y media.

10-15 Entrevista.

Answers will vary.

Tema 3 ¿Qué experiencia tiene Ud.?

10-16 No, ¡te equivocas!

1. vendedora, dependienta
2. secretaria, archivando
3. recepcionista
4. director, recursos
5. chófer
6. programadora
7. maestro, escuela

10-17 Entrevistas.

Un/a maestro/a de escuela primaria

¿Ha trabajado mucho con niños?

¿Ha dado clases en inglés y español?

¿Ha visto muchos libros para clases bilingües?

¿Ha hecho mucho teatro infantil?

¿Ha leído muchos cuentos indígenas para niños?

¿Ha tenido muchos problemas de disciplina?

¿Ha enseñado en una escuela primaria?

Un/a programador/a de computadoras

¿Ha diseñado muchas páginas Web?

¿Ha usado muchas bases de datos?

¿Ha programado una red de computadoras?

¿Ha escrito programas en UNIX?

¿Ha resuelto muchos problemas de virus?

10-18 Tengo que despedirla.

1. Ha dormido
2. Ha estado
3. Ha dejado
4. No ha aprendido
5. Ha llegado
6. Ha dicho
7. Ha roto
8. No ha hecho
9. No ha sido

10-19 Un colega mentiroso.

Yo...

He resuelto lo problemas con los clientes.

He diseñado la nueva página web.

He decir siempre la verdad.

He hecho la mayor parte del trabajo.

Nosotros...

Hemos tenido problemas con unos clientes. Hemos pagado demasiado por la publicidad.

Hemos escrito cosas equivocadas en la publicidad.

Hemos perdido unos clientes.

10-21 El día de Olga.

The illustrations should be numbered as follows:

__1__ (woman exercising)

__3__ (woman jogging in the park)

_Modelo 2__ (woman writing)

__6, 8__ (woman eating / watching T.V.)

__5__ (woman reading newspaper)

__10__ (woman leaving for work)

10-22 Entrevista.

Answers will vary.

Tema 4 ¿Qué han hecho?

10-23 ¿Quién lo ha hecho?

1. La directora de recursos humanos las ha recibido.

2. La supervisora los ha evaluado.

3. El programador los ha arreglado.

4. El recepcionista los ha recibido.

5. El diseñador gráfico los ha hecho.

6. La contadora los ha pagado.

10-24 ¿Quién se lo ha hecho a quién?

1. Pocos candidatos le han presentado una solicitud de empleo a la oficina de recursos humanos.

2. El secretario le ha traído los documentos para la reunión a la supervisora.

3. La supervisora les ha dado su evaluación a los empleados.

4. La contadora le ha pedido ayuda con su computadora al programador.

5. El secretario les ha distribuido el correo a todos los empleados.

6. El director de recursos humanos le ha ofrecido empleo a una de las candidatas.

7. La supervisora les ha dicho su decisión a los empleados.

8. La supervisora le ha devuelto los documentos al secretario para archivarlos.

9. El programador le ha hecho los cambios a la página web.

1. Pocos candidatos para el nuevo puesto se la han presentado (a la oficina de recursos humanos).

2. El secretario se los ha traído (a la supervisora).

3. La supervisora se la ha dado (a los empleados).

4. La contadora se la ha pedido (al programador).

5. El secretario se lo ha distribuido (a todos los empleados).

6. El director de recursos humanos se lo ha ofrecido (a una de las candidatas).

7. La supervisora se la ha dicho (a los empleados).

8. La supervisora se los ha devuelto (al secretario para archivarlos).

9. El programador se los ha hecho (a la página web).

10-25 ¿Qué ha realizado ya?

1. Sí, ya me he graduado de la preparatoria. / No, todavía no me he graduado de la preparatoria.

2. Sí, ya la he obtenido. / No, todavía no la he obtenido.

3. Sí, ya lo he terminado. / No, todavía no lo he terminado.

4. Sí, ya la he utilizado. / No, nunca la he utilizado.

5. Me he mudado un vez / dos veces / tres veces… durante los últimos cinco años. / No me he mudado durante los últimos cinco años.

6. Sí, lo he preparado recientemente. / No, no lo he preparado recientemente.

10-27 ¿Quién lo ha hecho?

a. No, la supervisora todavía no **los ha entrenado.**

b. No, el programador todavía no **la ha terminado.**

c. No, el secretario todavía no **los ha comprado.**

d. No, el director de recursos humanos todavía no **la ha publicado.**

e. No, la recepcionista todavía no **los ha visto.**

f. No, la contadora todavía no **lo ha calculado.**

g. No, el diseñador gráfico todavía no **la ha diseñado.**

10-28 Todavía no.

The illustrations should be numbered as follows:

__1__ (programmer)

__3__ (supervisor)

__Modelo__ (accountant)

__2__ (receptionist)

Tema 5 En el banco

10-29 Trámites bancarios.

1. préstamo	**4.** retiro	**7.** cuenta
2. crédito	**5.** débito	**8.** ahorros
3. pago	**6.** depósito	**9.** cargos

10-30 Reacciones.

1. Me alegro de que la policía haya arrestado a la persona que estaba utilizando el número de mi tarjeta de crédito.

2. Me alegro de que la persona que utilizó mi tarjeta de crédito haya devuelto todas las cosas que compró.

3. Me molesta que el banco me haya cobrado interés sobre los cargos de esa persona.

4. Me molesta que el banco haya perdido mi cheque de depósito directo.

5. Me alegro de que mi banco haya abierto una sucursal a cinco minutos de mi casa.

6. Me molesta que la nueva sucursal cerca de mi casa no tenga cajero automático.

7. Me alegro de que la nueva sucursal esté abierta hasta las siete de la tarde todos los días.

10-31 Consejos de una amiga.

1. conozca, hayas vivido

2. sepas, hayan estudiado

3. tengas, hayas hecho

4. hayas presentado, reciba

5. hayas cambiado, se vayan

6. haya decidido, llegues

10-33 Un préstamo.

— Temo que **no nos den el préstamo** para comprar el coche nuevo.

— ¿Por qué dudas que **nos presten** el dinero? Siempre **hemos pagado** todas nuestras cuentas a tiempo y tenemos **muy buen crédito**.

— No sé. Es mucho dinero. Nunca **le he pedido tanto dinero a** un banco.

— Me sorprende que **tengas tanto miedo. Has completado todos los formularios,** ¿verdad?

— Sí, voy a presentarlos en el banco esta mañana.

— Tenemos que hacerlo pronto. Me molesta que **la tasa de interés haya subido** esta semana, y **temo que vuelva a subir** pronto.

10-34 Sentimientos.

1. Me alegro de que…

2. Estoy contento/a de que…

3. Me alegro de que…

4. Me sorprende que…

5. Es bueno que…

6. Me molesta que…

7. Estoy contento/a de que…

8. Siento que…

Capítulo 11

Tema 1 ¿Cómo se informa Ud.?

11-1 Para todos los gustos.

| 1. noticiero | 3. programas de entrevistas | 5. televisión | 7. prensa | 9. pronóstico del tiempo |
| 2. noticias | 4. invitados | 6. documentales | 8. economía | 10. salas de chat |

11-2 Definiciones.

1. Un noticiero   4. Los programas de entrevistas

2. Los documentales   5. Las salas de chat

3. Un buscador

11-3 Conexiones.

1. Tengo un amigo del colegio que se llama Guzmán y que es presentador de noticias en una cadena de televisión.

2. Es una cadena de televisión en español en Estados Unidos que tiene una audiencia hispana muy grande.

3. Guzmán estudió la carrera de periodismo que le dio la oportunidad de entrar en el mundo de la televisión.

4. Primero, Guzmán estuvo trabajando en la cadena de televisión mexicana Azteca México que es una de las cadenas de televisión más importantes del país.

5. Guzmán hizo un trabajo excelente en la televisión mexicana que le abrió las puertas a la televisión hispana de Estados Unidos.

6. Guzmán tiene un trabajo de mucha responsabilidad que le permite conocer a personas muy interesantes del mundo de la economía y la política.

11-4 ¡Cuántos pronombres!

1. ¿Te informas de **lo que** pasa en el mundo? ¿Cuáles son las noticias **que** te interesan más?

2. ¿Cuáles son los invitados de los programas de entrevistas en **quienes** la audiencia está más interesada? ¿Estás interesado/a en **lo que** dicen esas personas?

3. Cuando lees la prensa, ¿quieres saber **lo que** está ocurriendo en los países de Latinoamérica o sólo lees las noticias **que** hablan de Estados Unidos?

4. ¿Cuáles son los programas de televisión **que** prefieren los estudiantes en tu universidad? ¿Te identificas con esos programas **que** son populares entre los estudiantes?

5. ¿Cuál es el buscador **que** más usan los estudiantes en tu universidad? ¿Controla tu universidad **lo que** pueden ver los estudiantes en Internet en las computadoras del campus?

Answers to the questions will vary.

11-6 ¿Qué ven? ¿Qué creen?

1. que ve con más frecuencia
2. quienes hablan de sus vidas personales
3. programas de entrevistas
4. que más ven los estudiantes en la universidad
5. lo que dan por la televisión
6. que enseñan los paisajes
7. documentales
8. quien le gusta ver la televisión
9. lo que ponen por las noches
10. que informan de las noticias locales y del mundo
11. noticieros

11-7 El show de Cristina.

1. Una presentadora
2. que
3. una anfitriona
4. que
5. El programa de entrevistas
6. lo que
7. una contribución
8. que

Tema 2 ¿Qué noticias locales y nacionales hay?

11-8 ¡Qué mundo!

1. que, violencia doméstica
2. que, inmigración, inmigrantes, quienes
3. que, pandillas
4. quienes, la asistencia social
5. desempleo, que

11-9 El mundo de la política.

1. presidente
2. elecciones
3. candidatos
4. sociedad
5. educación
6. desempleo
7. leyes
8. Congreso
9. jueces

11-10 La voz de la universidad.

1. Los estudiantes buscamos representantes políticos que **sean** honestos y que **comprendan** los problemas de la universidad.
2. Queremos líderes que **se preocupen** por las cuestiones de educación y que **miren** hacia el futuro de los jóvenes.
3. Los estudiantes tenemos preocupaciones que **afectan** a nuestro futuro y que **necesitan** ser oídas.
4. No hay ningún candidato en la actualidad que **entienda** nuestras preocupaciones ni que **responda** a nuestras peticiones.
5. Nuestros representantes universitarios son estudiantes que **conocen** muy bien las leyes y que **luchan** por los derechos de su gente.
6. Se necesitan más representantes en la política que **piensen** en las prioridades de los universitarios y **quieran** ayudarlos.

11-11 ¿Conocen a alguien que…?

1. ¿Conoces a algún candidato que hable español?
2. ¿Conocen a alguien que sea miembro de la pandilla de nuestro barrio?
3. ¿Hay muchas personas en tu ciudad que no tengan trabajo?
4. ¿Conocen a algunos votantes que estén descontentos con los resultados de las elecciones?
5. ¿Hay muchos estudiantes a quienes les preocupe la seguridad nacional?

11-12 En su universidad.

Answers will vary.

11-14 ¿Qué se necesita?

1. — ¿Cree que se necesitan leyes que **protejan** más a los ciudadanos?

— Sí, el gobierno debe dedicar más dinero a la **seguridad nacional.**

2. — ¿Cree que se necesitan leyes que **reduzcan** los impuestos?

— Sí, este país necesita una **reforma** de su economía.

3. — ¿Cree que se necesitan leyes que **mejoren** la situación de los trabajadores?

— Sí, porque hoy en día hay mucho **desempleo** en el país.

4. — ¿Cree que se necesitan leyes que **respondan** a las necesidades de las escuelas?

— Sí, la educación debe ser una **prioridad** del gobierno.

5. — ¿Cree que se necesitan iniciativas que **aumenten** la participación de las mujeres en la política?

— Sí, creo que una mujer candidata a **presidente** atraería a muchas votantes.

11-15 Hablando de política.

1. criminalidad	3. creen	5. noticias	7. robos	9. tema
2. pandillas	4. sean	6. empeora	8. encuesta	10. preocupe

Tema 3 ¿Qué noticias internacionales hay?

11-16 ¿Cuál es el problema?

1. La malnutrición	3. Una manifestación	5. Los indicadores económicos
2. Los terroristas	4. Un terremoto	6. La pobreza

11-17 Cuántos interrogantes.

1. llegará, ayuda humanitaria	3. impondrán, terrorismo	5. producirá, pobreza
2. Continuarán, protestas	4. revisará, recursos naturales	6. Habrá, inundaciones

11-18 No, no creo.

1. ¿Habrá más protestas contra la guerra?

2. ¿Invadirá Estados Unidos otro país?

3. ¿Mejorará el problema de la malnutrición en los países pobres?

4. ¿Impondrá el gobierno sanciones contra la devastación de la costa?

5. ¿Recortará el gobierno los impuestos en los próximos meses?

11-19 ¿Qué pasará si…?

1. Si se utilizan todos los recursos naturales, la Tierra morirá.

2. Nunca viviremos en paz, si no para el terrorismo.

3. Habrá más catástrofes naturales si continúa el calentamiento global.

4. Si las Naciones Unidas no llegan a un acuerdo, empeorarán las relaciones internacionales.

5. Los votantes protestarán contra las acciones del gobierno si el gobierno no revisa las leyes.

6. El mundo verá una mejora del medioambiente si los gobiernos imponen sanciones contra las empresas que contaminen.

11-20 Preguntas para el presidente.

Answers will vary.

11-22 Noticias internacionales.

1. titulares	**5.** reunirán	**9.** impondrá	**13.** empeorarán
2. protestaron	**6.** revisar	**10.** provocará	**14.** calentamiento global
3. amenazaron	**7.** terrorismo	**11.** indicadores económicos	
4. conflictos	**8.** acuerdos de paz	**12.** mejora	

11-23 Predicciones.

1. Los países del Oriente Medio **llegarán a un acuerdo de paz.**

2. Las víctimas de la catástrofe **recibirán ayuda humanitaria.**

3. Los representantes del Congreso **responderán a las prioridades de los ciudadanos.**

4. El terrorismo **amenazará la seguridad nacional.**

5. La economía y la seguridad nacional **serán las prioridades en el nuevo Congreso.**

6. Los sectores de tecnología y comunicaciones **mejorarán.**

7. La contaminación y la salud pública **empeorarán.**

8. Habrá más huracanes en Florida.

Tema 4 ¿Qué cambiará y cuándo?

11-24 ¿Será mejor el futuro?

1. En el futuro, los servicios de salud **estarán garantizados** para todos los ciudadanos y **habrá** más tratamientos para las enfermedades.

2. En los próximos años, los países **asegurarán** una mayor cooperación internacional y **aumentará la estabilidad económica.**

3. El futuro de la educación es muy bueno. Las instituciones **se beneficiarán** de los avances en tecnología y **habrá** más **oportunidades** para todos los estudiantes.

4. En las grandes ciudades se **reducirá** la contaminación y no **existirán** tantos **problemas ecológicos.**

5. En el futuro, las empresas **impondrán** leyes para la aceptación de trabajadores de distintas etnias y se **verá** más **diversidad** en los lugares de trabajo.

11-25 Imaginen.

1. Manejaremos coches eléctricos.

2. Trabajaremos desde casa con los avances en tecnología.

3. Habrá menos conflictos y más cooperación internacional.

4. Hablaremos por Internet y no usaremos el teléfono celular.

5. Tendremos aviones privados en vez de coches.

6. Habrá estabilidad y los índices de desempleo serán más bajos.

11-26 ¿Qué pasará cuando…?

1. Mientras los gobiernos no colaboren, habrá guerras.

2. Cuando haya elecciones, habrá muchos cambios.

3. Mientras continúen los avances en medicina, habrá curas para las enfermedades.

4. Hasta que no mejore la educación, no habrá oportunidades iguales para los jóvenes.

5. Cuando los países lleguen a un acuerdo, habrá verdadera cooperación internacional.

11-27 Circunstancias.

1. se casará, tenga

2. comprará, sepa

3. Se quedará, conozca

4. Estudiará, termine

5. Vivirá, ahorre

6. viajará, pague

7. estará, haga

Answers for the second part of the activity will vary.

11-29 La globalización.

1. **Habrá menos diversidad** con la globalización. – **en contra**

2. **Habrá más curas** para las enfermedades. – **a favor**

3. **La tecnología mejorará** las comunicaciones. – **a favor**

4. **Las comunicaciones serán** más impersonales. – **en contra**

5. **Habrá más cooperación** entre países. – **a favor**

6. **Los países ricos invadirán** a los pobres. – **en contra**

7. **Aumentará más** la pobreza. – **en contra**

8. **Habrá menos conflictos** internacionales. – **a favor**

9. **Habrá más comprensión** entre las sociedades. – **a favor**

10. **Los países perderán** parte de su identidad. – **en contra**

11-30 ¿Y tú?

Answers will vary.

Tema 5 ¿Será posible?

11-31 La fascinación por la farándula.

1. farándula   **2.** chismes   **3.** rupturas   **4.** telenovelas   **5.** acusados   **6.** rumor

11-32 ¡Cuántos chismes!

1. ¿Quién será el padre del niño?   **4.** ¿Habrá usado drogas durante su carrera?

2. ¿Se reconciliarán o se divorciarán?   **5.** ¿Tendrán un romance?

3. ¿Ganará las elecciones?

11-33 ¿Será cierto?

1. Será   **3.** Se divorciará   **5.** reducirá   **7.** Habrá   **9.** gustará   **11.** Llegará

2. Estará   **4.** grabará   **6.** estarán   **8.** publicarán   **10.** Tendremos   **12.** seremos

11-34 ¿Qué estarán haciendo?

1. Estarán protestando contra el aumento del precio de la matrícula.

2. Estará respondiendo a llamadas telefónicas de otros líderes internacionales.

3. Lo estarán arrestando (Estarán arrestándolo) por actividades ilegales.

4. Se estarán divorciando (Estarán divorciándose) legalmente.

5. Estará esperando la llegada de su bebé.

6. Estarán grabando episodios de la nueva temporada de *Tormento de Amor*.

11-36 Todo es mentira.

1. comprometedoras   **3.** asegura   **5.** embarazada   **7.** bebé   **9.** pareja   **11.** esperar

2. prensa   **4.** mentira   **6.** esperan   **8.** ruptura   **10.** acusaciones   **12.** telenovela

11-37 Suposiciones.

1. Estará estableciendo relaciones con el líder del país.

2. Estarán anunciando su boda.

3. Estará grabando una entrevista.

4. Estará recibiendo un premio.

5. Estará grabando una película.

Capítulo 12

Tema 1 ¿Qué les dijeron?

12-1 Preparativos.

1. solicitar
3. asesor
5. programa
7. tarjeta de identificación

2. matrícula
4. plan de estudios
6. alojamiento
8. matricularme

12-2 No, todavía no.

1. ¿Pagaste ya la matrícula?

2. ¿Obtuviste ya la tarjeta de identificación?

3. ¿Renovaste ya el pasaporte?

4. ¿Encontraste ya el alojamiento?

5. ¿Solicitaste ya la admisión?

6. ¿Revisaste ya los pasos a seguir para ser admitido?

12-3 ¿Ya tienes todo?

1. lo
3. él
5. él
7. lo
9. la
11. los
13. se
15. yo

2. me
4. te
6. lo
8. la
10. lo
12. los
14. La
16. Nosotras

12-4 Fui admitido en…

Answers will vary.

12-6 Con la asesora.

1. la
4. programa
7. la
10. las
13. varios

2. atender
5. fecha límite
8. planes de estudio
11. te
14. en el extranjero

3. me
6. solicitud
9. escoger
12. matricularme
15. te

12-7 Cuántas preguntas.

1. Sí, ya **lo escogí.**

2. Sí, ya **me los explicó.**

3. Sí, ya **lo reservé.**

4. No, todavía no **me lo han dicho.**

5. No, todavía no **la he obtenido.**

6. Sí, ya **me la enviaron.**

7. Sí, ya **me matriculé.**

Tema 2 ¿Podría Ud.…? ¿Debería…? ¿Le importaría a Ud.?

12-8 ¿Me podría…?

1. ¿Podría Ud. darme información sobre el programa de estudios en el extranjero?

2. ¿Podría Ud. asesorarme sobre el plan de estudios?

3. ¿Podría Ud. confirmarme las asignaturas obligatorias del programa?

4. ¿Podría Ud. decirme las asignaturas optativas del programa?

5. ¿Podría explicarme los pasos a seguir para ser admitido/a?

6. ¿Podría Ud. darme un impreso (un formulario) para solicitar la visa?

12-9 ¿Qué deberían…?

Answer may vary.

1. Debería obtener un impreso de admisión en el programa. Debería solicitar una tarjeta de identificación/una visa. Debería presentar un pasaporte vigente/un acta de nacimiento.

2. Debería presentar una carta de solvencia del banco/un acta de nacimiento/un pasaporte vigente. Debería obtener una visa.

3. Deberían obtener un impreso de admisión en el programa. Deberían presentar el certificado de secundaria.

12-10 Sería perfecto…

1. escribiría	**3.** podrías	**5.** iríamos	**7.** gustaría	**9.** pasaríamos	**11.** mostraría	**13.** pasarías
2. encantaría	**4.** preferiría	**6.** sería	**8.** deberías	**10.** Viajaríamos	**12.** probaríamos	**14.** volverías

12-11 ¿Qué dijeron?

1. la fecha límite de matrícula terminaría el primero de mayo para los estudiantes de nuevo ingreso.

2. los estudiantes extranjeros tendrían que presentar una fotocopia del pasaporte vigente.

3. sólo trece estudiantes recibirían ayuda económica para estudiar en el extranjero.

4. el Cónsul legalizaría el acta de nacimiento original sin ningún problema.

5. nos asesoraría sobre las asignaturas obligatorias y optativas que ofrece el programa.

12-13 Hola, buenas tardes.

1. podría	**4.** acta de nacimiento	**7.** original	**10.** sobre
2. debería	**5.** impreso	**8.** importaría	**11.** admisiones
3. vigente	**6.** legalizada	**9.** enviar	**12.** registro

12-14 Un sistema perfecto.

1. serían	**3.** tendrían	**5.** tendrían pocos estudiantes, podrían participar
2. pasarían un semestre	**4.** estarían	**6.** serían buenas

Tema 3 ¿Es necesario?

12-15 Nacionalidades.

1. Frida Kahlo y Diego Rivera fueron mexicanos.

2. Eva Perón fue argentina.

3. Gabriel García Márquez es colombiano.

4. Gloria Estefan es cubana.

5. Julia Álvarez es estadounidense.

6. Pedro Almodóvar es español.

a. gustaría   **b.** hablaría   **c.** preguntaría

The statements in the last section will vary.

12-16 Se necesitan...

1. atiendan   **2.** proporcionen   **3.** tramiten   **4.** revisen   **5.** entiendan   **6.** tengan

12-17 Tramitar la visa.

1. Es importante que no tramiten la visa en el último momento en el consulado o la embajada.

2. Más vale que saquen fotos tamaño pasaporte antes de ir al consulado o la embajada.

3. Es necesario que presenten un estado de su cuenta personal o de la cuenta de sus padres.

4. Les recomiendo que rellenen la solicitud de visa con cuidado.

5. Es necesario que renueven la visa en caso de permanecer en el país.

6. Es importante que no sean impacientes.

12-18 Con tal de que...

1. Podrás permanecer en el país con tal que renueves la visa.

2. No escogerás el programa de estudios hasta que no hables con tu asesor.

3. No obtendrás una tarjeta de identificación a menos que te presentes en sus oficinas.

4. Podrás estudiar en el extranjero con tal que entregues la solicitud en la fecha límite.

5. Deberás tramitar una visa a menos que seas ciudadano del país.

6. El acta de nacimiento no será válida a menos que esté legalizada por el Cónsul.

12-20 ¿Hay alguien que...?

1. — ¿Hay funcionarios de inmigración que **hablen español**?

    — Sí, hay muchos funcionarios de inmigración que **hablan español.**

2. — ¿Hay países que **no tengan** consulado cerca de Miami?

    — Sí, hay varios países que **no tienen** consulado cerca de Miami.

3. — ¿Hay consulados que **no tramiten visas**?

    — No, todos los consulados **tramitan visas.**

4. — ¿Hay pasaportes que **no tengan foto**?

    — No, todos los pasaportes **tienen foto.**

5. — ¿Hay muchos inmigrantes que **soliciten la ciudadanía estadounidense**?

    — Sí, hay muchos inmigrantes que **solicitan la ciudadanía estadounidense.**

12-21 Dudo que...

1. permanezca   **2.** me prolonguen   **3.** me den   **4.** sea   **5.** pueda

Tema 4 ¿Qué le dijeron que hiciera?

12-22 En la Oficina de Inmigración.

1. (Soledad) hizo una cita por teléfono.   **3.** Hizo cola y esperó su turno.   **5.** Completó los formularios.

2. Acudió a la hora prevista.   **4.** Habló con el funcionario.   **6.** Entregó los documentos

12-23 ¡Vaya día!

1. papeleo   **3.** cita   **5.** hacer cola   **7.** acudir   **9.** tarifas

2. esperar   **4.** prevista   **6.** domicilio   **8.** funcionarios   **10.** visa

12-24 Entonces, ¿qué pasó?

1. me diera una cita   **3.** mostrara mi domicilio   **5.** volviera mañana con la documentación

2. me dijera los documentos   **4.** necesitara un comprobante de domicilio   **6.** tramitara correctamente mi visa

12-25 ¿Qué les dijo?

1. estuvieran preparados para el comienzo del curso

2. acudieran a la reunión de información para estudiantes extranjeros

3. se presentaran en la oficina para obtener una tarjeta de identificación

4. se matricularan para las clases del otoño

5. no realizaran el papeleo en el último momento

6. no pagaran las tarifas de matrícula después de la fecha límite

12-27 Un servicio valioso.

1. inmigración **3.** realizar   **5.** permanecer **7.** pasaporte   **9.** funcionarios **11.** tarifas   **13.** ciudadanos

2. acuden   **4.** renovar   **6.** solicitar   **8.** esperan su turno **10.** formularios **12.** proporciona **14.** residentes

12-28 Expectativas diferentes.

1. Quique – tuviera   **3.** Quique – atendiera   **5.** Olga – asesoraran   **7.** Quique - diera

2. Olga – fuera   **4.** Quique – proporcionara   **6.** Olga – realizaran   **8.** Olga - hubiera

Tema 5 Les agradecería…

12-29 Estimados señores.

1. Estimados **3.** solicitar   **5.** fechas límite **7.** acerca de   **9.** alojamiento **11.** Con referencia **13.** A la espera de

2. dirijo   **4.** Quisiera   **6.** agradecería   **8.** confirmar   **10.** tarifas   **12.** obtener   **14.** atentamente

12-30 Soluciones para Arancha.

1. Si no pudiera estudiar en el extranjero sin perder mi beca, escogería un programa de voluntariado en el extranjero durante el verano.

2. Si no pudiera permanecer en el país porque mi visa no está vigente, prolongaría la visa en el consulado.

3. Si no pudiera tramitar mi solicitud de residencia hoy porque hay una cola tremenda, tramitaría la solicitud por Internet.

4. Si no pudiera hablar con mi asesor en sus horas de oficina, trataría de hacer una cita a otra hora.

5. Si no pudiera hacer amistades fácilmente porque soy muy tímida, participaría en más actividades sociales de la universidad.

12-31 Hipótesis.

1. recibieras   2. enojaría   3. probara   4. quisieras   5. entregara   6. agradecería

12-32 Si pudiera…

Answers will vary.

12-34 En respuesta a su carta.

1. Estimada   4. Adjunto   7. acuda
2. En referencia 5. previsto   8. atenderán
3. quisiera   6. tramitar   9. Atentamente

12-35 ¿Cómo reaccionarías?

1. Si no pudiera renovar mi visa, no haría nada.

2. Si tuviera que esperar en una cola muy larga para tramitar mi visa, me quejaría.

3. Si mi asesor me ayudara a escoger los cursos, se lo agradecería.

4. Si la oficina tramitara mi solicitud incorrectamente, me enojaría.